RED DIRT WHITE BONES

A REPLACEMENT GIRL MYSTERY

GREG FIELD

Red Dirt White Bones

Copyright © 2014 by Greg Field

No part of this book may be reproduced or transmitted in any form or by any means, electronic or mechanical, including photocopy, recording, or any information storage and retrieval system, without permission in writing from the author or his agents, except by a reviewer who may quote brief passages in a critical review to be printed in a magazine, or newspaper, or their electronic equivalent, or electronically transmitted on radio or television.

All persons, places, and organizations in this book except those clearly in the public domain are fictitious, and any resemblance that may seem to exist to actual persons, places, events, or organizations, living, dead, or defunct, is purely coincidental.

All brand names and product names used in this book are trademarks, registered trademarks, or trade names of their respective holders. We are not associated with any product or vendor mentioned.

This is a work of fiction.

ISBN 978-0-9860975-1-5

Printed in the United States of America

RED DIRT WHITE BONES

1

FRIDAY

The bones were white against the red soil. At the bottom of the trench two anthropologists used paintbrushes to gently peel away the clay covering the remains. To one side of the neatly cut six-foot-deep hole a large cone of dirt settled. The bucket of the backhoe rested on the other side.

Detective Kai sat on the bucket and watched them work. The backhoe operator, out of his cab, inched towards the edge, focusing on the young blonde female in khaki shorts bent over in the hole.

"They're not that old," the senior anthropologist said over his shoulder.

"How can you tell?" called out Kai.

"This dress. It's polyester."

Kai made a call on his cell phone. He got a voice message and left directions to the site. The sky was a pure blue. When he looked out to the horizon he could see the Honolulu skyline beyond Pearl Harbor. Every few minutes a plane from the mainland made a wide 180-degree turn, flying low overhead for the approach to Honolulu

International.

Sunlight dropped straight down into the hole. The black polyester dress was stained from the dirt but had not deteriorated with time. This was not an ancient burial ground. When the backhoe operator uncovered human remains he'd stopped digging, pulled his bucket to the side, and called his supervisor. By Hawai'i state law an anthropologist must accompany all large construction projects in the event they uncover bones. If they are determined to be ancestral bones, they must be respectfully reinterred—buried again on site or moved to another location.

"So, do I get my hole back?" A man in Dockers and a sweat-soaked khaki shirt approached Kai. Red dirt powdered the lower part of his pants legs. His neck was burned and creased from the sun and his bulbous nose tended towards pink.

"Not today. Maybe Monday, maybe the day after. It's a crime scene now."

"Oh, great. This is why you people never get anything done. You and your damn bones." He went on muttering and cursing.

The contractor was from the mainland. The politicians promised new jobs when the rail project was pushed through. Many of the choice contracts went to companies with experience building rail lines, and were all from out of state. They hired their own laborers, flying them in from other parts of the country.

The man in khaki rounded up his backhoe operator and they drove off in a jeep.

"A button," the young anthropologist said, her face glowing from the sun. She pointed to it with the handle of her brush and looked up at Detective Kai as if she were giving him a gift. "A white button." She was very limber and her long legs easily straddled the bones as she crouched over them.

He nodded.

They would find a row of them. The plastic buttons outlasted the cotton blouse they'd been attached to.

The detective called down. "The dress. Could it be a jumper?"

The senior anthropologist cleared away more dirt and touched a drop of water to it. "Yes, you could call it a jumper. A navy-blue jumper."

The medical examiner's van rumbled up the dirt road and pulled in behind the detective's SUV. A tech got out from behind the wheel and strode to the hole's edge, looked down, then shook his head and retreated to the back of the van. A middle-aged woman stepped out of the passenger's side and walked to the edge of the hole. She was in a skirt and high heels and took short steps to traverse the uneven ground. Doctor Rajastani, Senior Medical Examiner, looked into the hole. A lock of hair slid off one shoulder and obscured her face. She pushed her hair back and looked at the detective over large dark glasses. "You let them touch my body."

What he wouldn't do to touch her body. Long dark hair hung down past her rounded rump. She had red painted lips, amber skin, and emerald eyes. Like a traffic light, her lips said *'stop'* but her eyes said—she pushed the glasses up her nose.

"I told them not to move the bones," he said. "Just the dirt enough to verify these were modern materials."

The anthropologists had stopped working and were looking up, no doubt sensing a shift in the pecking order.

"Which they've done. That's why you called me." Her

fists were on her hips, her feet apart. He could feel the daggers from behind the dark glasses. She looked into the hole. "You can step out now. I'll take it from here." The ME walked carefully back to the van, climbed in the rear door, and slammed it behind her.

The anthropologists climbed the ladder and pulled it up behind them. They gathered their tools and prepared to leave. The young anthropologist, probably a grad student working for the Bishop Museum for the summer, seemed to linger. She was slender, with a sunburned nose and a smudge of dirt on her forehead.

She stepped close to him and said softly, "Some of us in the Anthropology department meet up at Anna's. Upstairs, around ten."

Anna's was a bar near the university. It served cheap drinks and had a live band most nights. Conversation was near impossible and the dancing frenetic. On a good night you'd go home smelling of beer and sticky from your own sweat. On a *really* good night you wouldn't go home alone. Why not? It was Friday night. Kai took off his sunglasses and held her gaze. He nodded and gave her just a little bit of a smile. It was enough to make her cheeks turn pink.

The grad student joined her colleague in their Jeep Cherokee and headed down the dirt track.

The ME assistant dropped a new ladder into the hole. He laid a tarp next to the hole and put several boxes, each a foot square, on the tarp.

Dr. Rajastani, stepped out of the back of the van. She now wore dark blue coveralls with the sleeves rolled up past her elbows, and Nikes on her feet. A hair net and a baseball cap covered her head.

"You know better, Detective," she said without looking towards him. "Always in a hurry, aren't you?" She climbed down the ladder and looked at the bones. "It'll be a couple of hours before we get them out and back to the lab. I won't be able to tell you anything until then."

"I'll get you started," Kai said. "The victim was female and in her teens. She was a Catholic—most likely."

Dr. Raj put her hands on her hips and looked up at him, her head tilted as if to say, *'how the hell do you know?'*

"The navy-blue jumpsuit is a parochial school uniform. Saint Teresa's—a high school over near Wai'alae."

Did she almost smile?

"I'll call you later with an ID." He winked and headed to his car, slipping his sunglasses back on.

Dust had settled on his windshield. He hit the sprinkler and the wiper swept dry arcs across the glass.

2

The Subaru Outback, Kai's personally owned vehicle and not a police issue, was a few years old. It was small and efficient but large enough to keep his surfboard inside. He drove the dirt track until it connected to the local road.

Sugar plantations dominated this area for over a century. But the economics of sugar required cheap land, cheap labor, and plentiful water—three commodities that were increasingly difficult to find. Hawai'i sugar production was no longer competitive with third-world countries. The large landowner could realize greater returns from another more profitable crop—perhaps the only crop requiring more water than sugar—single-family homes.

This part of the Ewa Plain was still under development. Construction crews worked on a block of houses. Exposed steel studs and plywood roof decks revealed the innards. Further up the street finished homes still awaited landscaping. As he drove, he passed an area where a half-dozen model homes were being shown. Here the landscaping was remarkable—very tropical, with mature, feathery palms, and large dark-green leaved plants bordering sprinkler-wet, glistening green lawns. Without an irrigation system, all this would wither and die. But for the purpose of selling the homes the landscaping was rich, verdant, and well tended.

The trench he'd just visited was one of a series of excavations for the pylons of the new rail system to bring commuters from the Second City to downtown Honolulu. Traffic along the only highway to the leeward side of the island was among the worst commutes in the nation. Heading back to town midday was not a problem and he'd be at St. Teresa's High School in forty minutes or less.

He'd check in with his lieutenant after he'd talked to the school administrators. Any sooner and he might get pulled back into the office and he'd spend the rest of the day behind a desk. If he timed it right he'd have a good idea of the identity of the bones by the end of the day and he could call it quits from there.

Kai pulled into the small parking lot—no empty spaces. He parked at the end of a bus loading zone, put the magnetic blue police dome on his car roof, and followed the sign towards the school administration. The mission style campus—cream stucco walls and red roof tile—seemed like a small cloister. He found himself in a central courtyard with a fountain as its focus. Saint Teresa stood stone still in the center of the gurgling water. Her hands pulled at her robes, her head back in a swoon, eyelids drooped as if caught in intense pain—or the throes of orgasm. An arrow pierced her heart. He knew how she felt.

He stepped through the doors labeled 'office' and

removed his sunglasses. In the moment it took for his eyes to adjust to the relative dark he heard a soft voice ask, "May I help you?"

His eyes found the woman behind the counter and he displayed his police identification and badge as he approached. "I'm with the Honolulu Police Department. May I speak with the principal?"

She returned a matronly smile. "I'll see if Dr. Jeffers can meet with you. Won't you have a seat?"

He preferred to stand. He had memories of waiting on a bench like the one he'd been waived towards while the principal took his time getting to him. He'd used the same technique in interrogations—placing a subject in a room with nothing to do, no stimulation, seated, no control over their environment, then suddenly entering the room and standing over them. The principals had always towered over him and the impression never left him. He always spilled to them.

A tall woman approached him. She was in her fifties with short salt and pepper hair. She'd skipped the makeup—he doubted she ever needed it. She wore a grey frock—not a nun's habit but not street clothes either. "I'm Doctor Jeffers, Dean of Students. How can I help you detective—?"

He held up his identification. "Detective Kaipupule Ahuna-Aki."

She glanced down at his identification, then leveled her blue eyes to his.

"I'm investigating human remains found today out in Ewa. The bones were surrounded by a navy-blue jumper. It reminded me of St. Teresa's uniform. I'm wondering if there'd been a disappearance of a student—not recently, but something from at least several years ago."

The bell rang before she could answer. In a moment the hallway was filled with teenage girls in white blouses and navy-blue pleated skirts. They navigated around the two on their way to their next class.

Dr. Jeffers appeared thoughtful. "A navy-blue jumper, you say. We changed our uniforms to a white blouse and navy skirt some years ago." She held out her hand to suggest he take a look around him. "We haven't had jumpers in—oh, ten years. It was one of the first things I did when I became Dean of Students. But if you're certain about the jumper, it *is* possible the remains are of a former student."

The rush of students around them was ebbing. She waited as if an inner clock told her to pause, and in a moment the bell rang. The halls were now perfectly clear.

"Let's walk this way."

They walked side by side under the arched cloisters surrounding the central courtyard.

"A few years before I came to St. Teresa, a girl went missing. I'm afraid I don't remember her name, but we can find it easy enough. Her teachers were very fond of her and spoke of her long after—well, she was never found."

"Can I speak with one of her teachers?"

"None of the teachers from that time are still here. But our librarian—she was, and I'm certain she can tell you about the girl you're looking for." She'd directed him to the library and indicated the door. He opened it and held it for her.

The library was cool and again his eyes adjusted back to the low light levels. To one side was a counter, and beyond it, rows of tall book shelves. The stacks were against the wall. In the center of the room a few students sat quietly at long tables working on assignments. An older woman stood over a young girl seated at the table and pointed to one of the books in front of her. This woman more closely fit his image of a nun—she wore a coarse white tunic with a dark shawl pinned to her hair. She looked up as they approached.

"Sister Rosa," Dr. Jeffers said in a hushed voice. "This is Detective Kai—I'm sorry, I've forgotten your name."

"Detective Kai will do."

"Detective Kai is conducting an investigation, and you may be able to assist him."

Sister Rosa looked up at him through thick bifocals. They stepped away from the student. "I shall do what I can."

"You're in good hands with Sister Rosa, Detective Kai. Please stop by my office on you way out." Dr. Jeffers left the library.

Sister Rosa shrugged her shoulders. "How can I help the police?"

"Dr. Jeffers told me a number of years ago, before she came here, a girl went missing."

Sister Rosa closed her eyes and made a slow sign of the cross. When she opened her eyes the sadness was apparent. Her shoulders slumped and she let out a long deep breath. She led him to the counter and took a desk chair behind it. She nodded her head slowly. "That was fifteen years ago."

He took the chair opposite her. "Is there anything you can tell me about her, beginning with her name."

"Lana." She rolled her chair to a nearby bookshelf and plucked a volume from a set of school year books. "We had her for a year and a half—before she was taken. This is the yearbook for the class that graduated the year she disappeared. She was a sophomore, but she's in a lot of pictures." She flipped through the book and pointed to a group shot of a production of *Romeo and Juliet*. Although six other persons were in the picture, the photographer had focused on Juliet, played by Lana.

She was a beautiful girl just at the cusp of womanhood. Her dark hair was pulled back in a braid intertwined with ribbon that hung to her waist. Another smaller braid crossed her forehead at the hairline in a very Elizabethan style. Her almond shaped eyes suggested the mixed lineage common in Hawai'i. She could have been Latina or Middle Eastern or a *haole* girl with a good tan.

He spotted her in another photo, and then a third. The camera and the stage lighting captured the high cheekbones and wide jaw. Her long neck led the eye to the open bodice, accentuated by the high waist of the costume. But it was more than just her lithe figure. He was drawn to her expressive face, full strong lips, and those eyes.

"At the end of the year we made a video—a compilation of some of her best scenes. We called it a 'tribute.' We didn't want to use the word 'memorial,' but by then most of us had lost hope of ever seeing her again. I put it up on YouTube. Would you like to see it? It's about five minutes long."

"Sure."

Sister Rosa awoke the computer on her desk and quickly cued up the clip. She handed him a set of earphones. "You can listen with these."

Sister Rosa's hands were trembling. She got up from her chair. "I—I'll just be in the back." A tear splashed on the desktop. She held a handkerchief to her nose and retreated to the reference section.

Kai started the video and brought it up to full screen. White letters on a black screen: "Lana Reynolds," the date of her birth—"forever in our hearts."

She was born the same year as he. They would have been about the same age, both sophomores studying the same things but at different schools.

The black screen faded and the first shot was of Lana looking directly at him. "Hi, I'm Lana," she said to him. She wore an oversized work shirt—faded to a soft, light heather. The top two buttons were open, but not in a provocative way. Behind her a theater set was partly constructed and he got the impression she'd just taken a break from painting it. She smiled and said thoughtfully, "I want to be…" She took on a mischievous smile.

Jump to a scene from *West Side Story*: She was part of a chorus, her hair with a loose wave and a curl that fell across her forehead. In song they debated the virtues of New York versus San Juan. Then a fade to a duet with Lana and a boy her age. They were on the fire escape of a New York tenement. She looked deep into his eyes and touched his cheek lightly. It was a scene of two young persons falling in love. Kai could see the love, and yearned to feel that kind of love himself.

There was a great variety to the clips. Some were drama scenes from a play or movie, while others were comedy pieces. The video ended with the full interview that started the piece. Looking straight at the camera—straight at him—Lana said, "I want to be—an interpreter of feelings, a painter with motion and words, a dancer who can stand still and depict the movement in my mind—and my heart. I want to be the girl next door, and the girl you wish was next door. And I want to take the emotions you've felt, and all the ones you've been afraid to feel, and put them out where you can see them, respect them, or cringe in horror. I want you to see me completely so we understand who we are—and who I am." She laughed. "And I want to be very, very good at it." She jumped up and ran away from the camera, glancing over her shoulder with a laugh, and ran through the darkened set.

The video faded to black, but then a solo voice, her voice, sang without accompaniment. A long shot of Lana alone on a darkened stage with a single spot on her, the camera slowly circling in on her. She sang with certainty of a place and a time—and he believed her. Fade to black.

He replayed the video. This time he paused at specific scenes, and noted the time in the lower corner. He looked in the yearbook and saw certain pictures he wanted more information on. Although he hadn't heard her he had the sense Sister Rosa was behind him. Without turning, he said, "Her disappearance really affected you."

Sister Rosa sat in her chair. Her eyes were red. "Yes, very much so."

"You were more to her than the librarian."

She nodded. "In those days I taught English literature and I was the faculty mentor for the drama club. The first day she read aloud in class I felt it. Her first audition I knew it—we all knew. She had it, in a way I'd never seen before. When she came in a room your eyes were on her. When she spoke, when she whispered, you were listening, yearning to hear. Every teacher hopes to have that one— that one special student you *knew* would make it. Lana was that one.

"When she disappeared, well, I prayed. I prayed for her return, and after a while when it seemed hopeless, I prayed for me, for my faith. I'd lost her and I was in danger of losing my faith in God. How could He let this happen? How could a loving, caring God take away the one among us who was like a mirror of His light? Her innocence was gone and so was mine. I couldn't teach. I couldn't guide the ones who needed guidance from me.

"My confessor recommended I take time off. I did, but my thoughts turned even darker. He referred me to a special counselor, a psychiatrist who is in our church. It took a year before I could come back—but not as a teacher. I would never be able to get so close to a child again. I simply couldn't. And so I've been the librarian ever since."

Her head hung down and she looked at her fingers pressing in slow succession the beads of the rosary. He reached over and put his hand on hers. He saw her try to smile. He'd seen this done in an interview and had adopted it for moments like this.

"And my faith in Him—it is not as it was. The One I love has cheated on me and I'll never be able to give the trust I once had. That's a hard thing to say. I will never know the workings of God's mind." She looked up. "Thank you, Detective Kai. You're very kind to listen." She looked to the screen of the computer. "You have other questions for me?"

"There are a few kids who frequently show up in pictures with Lana." He pointed to an example in the yearbook. "Could these be special friends?"

Sister Rosa looked at the book. "Yes. The one with the long blond hair, that's her best friend, Angela Cooper. And the dark haired girl is Edra Monis. They were close too. But she had a lot of friends. Everyone *wanted* to be her friend."

"In the plays that you did, there are male parts, but Saint Teresa's is all girls?"

"Well, now we do have some boys—four. Not even enough for a basketball team, the poor guys. But yes, then we were all girls. When we did a play we'd partner with

Saint John of the Cross. It's just down the road a few blocks. They're a small school—all boys."

"There's a boy I saw in a few of the pictures. He's not leading man material, but he shows up a few times."

"Not leading man material. You were a rascal in school, I can tell." She chuckled and shook her head. "That's Zack Pizzo. He was a couple inches shorter than Lana, and skinny as a rail. His parents couldn't afford orthodontic work and his teeth were all crooked. He got a double dose of acne and wore thick glasses. He probably *wished* he could play Romeo to her Juliet, or Tony in *West Side Story*. He was never more than an extra in a play, but he was *very* helpful back stage. If anybody was Lana's boyfriend it was he."

Kai wrote the name down in his notebook. He used the camera in his phone to take a picture of the shots with Pizzo and Lana's other friends. "There seemed to be a lot of plays that she was in. You mentioned *Romeo and Juliet* and *West Side Story*, but there were several other productions I didn't recognize."

"She was quite a force. She had so much energy, and just being around her, your energy increased. It was her idea for the drama club to produce a weekly TV show. A half-hour full of skits and songs. Sometimes drama, sometimes comedy. They'd take scenes from movies or plays. It was a great idea, and it made Lana even more popular. I mean she walked away with two plum leads in two years—she deserved them. Her auditions just blew away the competition. But you could see how it might leave other girls feeling like they'd always be in her shadow. The weekly program was a way for others to get leading roles too. She directed a lot of the vignettes—and everyone wanted to have her direct. She was an actor's director. She made the actor look good."

"Were there any girls who thought that maybe with Lana around they'd never get their shot?"

"Girls at that age are very competitive—very cliquish. I imagine there was some of what you say. I honestly don't remember anyone in particular, but I can't rule it out."

He pointed to a medium shot of Juliet. "What's this on her left hand? You can see it again from another angle."

Sister Rosa looked closer. "Oh, that. Late in the fall of her freshman year Lana broke her arm. It was just a week or two before *Romeo and Juliet* was going to go on. She had a cast on her arm, but the costume covered it up almost completely. Her mother made the costumes—she was a designer with her own clothing line at Liberty House. See how she made the sleeves long and droopy at the end? It looks very Elizabethan, but really it was to conceal the part of the cast that comes down over the palm. Very creative, if you ask me."

"Sister Rosa, you've been a big help. Thank you for your time."

"The police asked a lot of questions—but then nothing. Why are you asking questions now?"

"We've found bones in an excavation in Ewa. I think it may be Lana."

The wind seemed to leave her and a look of desperation came across her face. Was all the old trauma coming back to her? She asked softly, "Will you catch the person who did this?"

"I can't make that promise. I'll go back to my lieutenant and show him what I've got. If he feels there's enough new material to reopen the investigation then he'll make a decision who to put on it."

"But he might decide not to."

"That's right. Having the bones is important. It establishes that a homicide took place, but it may not give us anything *new* to work with. It's been fifteen years."

She dropped her head. "I understand. I shouldn't put my faith that anything will happen. And it may not be *you* who gets the case. It's all out of your hands." She faked a smile then looked away. "Thank you, Detective Kai."

He rose from his seat. The sister was still looking away, deep into the library, as if she could see through the far wall, as if she could see back fifteen years.

Kai left the library and followed the cloister back to the entrance to the administration offices. He called the Medical Examiner's office. It went to message.

"Doctor Raj, this is Kai. The bones you picked up in Ewa. Please check the lower left arm for a healed break. Lana Reynolds went missing fifteen years ago. A year before, she broke her arm." He hung up.

He entered the administration wing and tapped on the open door of the Dean of Students. Doctor Jeffers looked up and waved him in and to the chair opposite her desk.

"Was Sister Rosa helpful?"

"Very. But as I explained to her, the call whether to reopen the investigation is above my pay grade."

"If there is anything that we can do to help—anything. Please let me know."

"There is one thing. I know we have it in our files, but you may be able to access it faster. Do you have an address for Lana Reynolds? She was a Sophomore fifteen years ago."

Doctor Jeffers turned to her computer and after a few seconds wrote the address on a Post-it and handed it to Kai.

They stood at the same time. She extended her hand and he shook it. Her hand was warm and he looked deep into her blue eyes.

As he walked back to his car, the school bell rang. Students filed out of the rooms but in a more excited way then before. It must have been the final bell. Girls coursed all around him chatting excitedly. He remembered himself at this age, and his sister who was a couple years behind him. A school bus was pulled up to the rear bumper of his car. He unlocked the door, took the blue bubble light from the roof, and put it on the back seat.

"Detective Kai." Sister Rosa was threading her way to him through the flow of girls. She held the yearbook in her hands. "Detective Kai, I want you to hold on to this—just in the event."

He took the book from her. She was putting pressure on him, but decision-making was out of his control. He got in his car and drove slowly through the crush of girls walking off campus. A few blocks away, he turned into Zippy's and went into the fast food side of the restaurant. While waiting for his chili and rice, he took the Post-it out of his pocket and looked at it. The address was about half a mile away.

He was part way through his chili when his phone vibrated. The image of Dr. Raj appeared on the screen. He stared at it for a moment. She'd just started at the M.E.'s office and he'd taken her picture when he entered her contact information. She grabbed his phone and frowned at the picture. She pulled off her white lab coat revealing a lilac blouse, removed her glasses and surgical cap, and shook out her hair. Holding the phone at arm's length, she moistened her lips, tipped her head so that a lock of thick black hair fell across her forehead, and leveled those dark-lined, green eyes at the lens. It was the kind of thing high school girls did—and that was as far as they'd gotten.

He touched the screen. "Kai."

"The subject had a spiral fracture of her lower left arm. It was set and healed."

"A spiral fracture?"

"Yes, this occurs when there is a torqueing or twisting force."

"As when a right-handed person grabs the left arm of the person they're facing and the person resists?"

"Yes, but a spiral fracture is not indicative of abuse. We see more of them from sports accidents, so don't jump to conclusions."

"Thank you, Doctor."

Just then a waitress called out an order to be picked up.

"Where are you?" She could hear the background noise.

"Zippy's on Wai'alae."

"Eating chili with rice, no doubt." He could hear the judgment in her voice.

"You know me too well," he said, but really they knew each other not well at all. They were both quiet on the line as if they recognized the irony of his comment and knew it could easily be otherwise—but neither took the next step.

"We'll check her dental records to confirm, but as of now, Jane Doe is Lana Reynolds. Will you make the notification?"

She knew the procedure. She'd just needed something to say. "I'll have to check in first. It will be the loo's call."

"Call me—if you need anything." She hung up.

He took his half-eaten chili back to his car. He called

in. "Lieutenant, the bones out in Ewa, they belong to a teenage girl who went missing fifteen years ago, name of Lana Reynolds."

"How'd you get to that?"

"I recognized the school uniform—it held up all these years. I stopped by the school and they showed me pictures of the girl. She had a healed broken arm consistent with the remains. Doctor Raj called the I.D. pending dental records."

"Alright. Come on in. You're still restricted to desk duty. We've got more back files to be digitized. You can spend a couple hours doing that."

"I'm just a few blocks from the parent's address. I could make the notification."

"That can wait until we get more from the M.E. Until then we don't know any more than we did before the bones were found."

"We know the doer had access to a backhoe. Six feet—that's plenty deep."

"Alright, but don't say we have any new leads. We have remains that *may* be hers. We need release of dental records. That's all. We don't want to open up old wounds."

"Got it. I'll just get some general info while I'm there."

"Don't spend much time on it. I'll assign the case after the weekend. Just finish up the day on it."

"Okay."

"And by the way, you had someone looking for you."

Kai sighed. This past month he'd been interviewed by an Officer Involved Shooting Board, a Professional Standards Board, three insurance companies, a Prosecuting Attorney, even a shrink to assess his actions and his readiness for duty. "Who was it this time?"

"A recruiter from Baldwin PD." Baldwin, Washington

was a medium size town undergoing a population surge. An aeronautics company near the town won a big military contract, and several thousand new jobs—from engineers to assembly line workers—would be created. The population was expected to double in five years. Ten thousand single-family houses were being built, new shopping centers planned, infrastructure and services needed to expand quickly. The small police department was actively and openly recruiting academy trained officers from small cities where the pay was below the national average—like the Honolulu PD. It was a cost effective way to get trained, seasoned officers, especially detectives. The recruiters weren't allowed in the building, but they hung out by the authorized personnel entrance. "I told the buzzards they could have you. I even filled out the application for you. All you got to do is sign. It's sitting on your desk."

"That was thoughtful of you."

"Anything to clear the squad of you. I'll come to your place and pack your bags if it will get you out of here. You know you'll be happier some place else."

3

He cruised down 17th Avenue looking for the house number. This was an older residential neighborhood with small, single-wall houses—single-story structures that relied on the strength of ¾ inch thick vertical siding to carry the load of the hip roof.

These modest, unembellished homes bore similarities in design because of the limitations of their construction. The thin walls offered no insulation—air conditioning was via the jalousie windows and the ceiling fans centered in every room. The houses, usually with an open carport to one side, were on small lots and close together.

As he rolled down the street looking for the house number, he noticed a mailbox at the curb with one-inch reflective letters spelling "ONIS." The front yard featured weeds of varying heights, half obscuring the bright colors of children's toys—a red big-wheel tricycle, a yellow beach pail, a nude brown doll—all securely behind a four-foot high chain link fence.

Midway up the street he found the address and parked. He opened a port-a-file on the back seat and found a blank standard release form, folded it, and put it in his pocket. He looked the house over. The front door was open, with just the screen door pulled closed. He passed a low rock wall with no gate, and walked up the path to the front steps and knocked on the wall to the side of the door.

He heard shuffling inside. A woman in her fifties approached from the dark interior. She wore baggy shorts and t-shirt and was barefoot. "Yes? Who is it?"

"Hello. Mrs. Reynolds?"

"Who are you?"

"Detective Ahuna-Aki, Honolulu Police Department."

She looked through the screen at his ID.

"The Reynolds haven't lived here in, oh, thirteen or fourteen years."

"Do you have a forwarding address?"

"I did. I used to get their mail from time to time, but not for a long while. I'm sure I don't have it anymore."

"Have you heard any of your neighbors talk about them—like they might've kept in touch?"

She shrugged. "No. They lived here a long time ago."

"Thank you for your time."

He followed the short front walk to his car and put his sunglasses on. A grey Caravan passed and he tracked it with his eyes. It pulled into the driveway of the unkempt house at the far end of the street. A woman got out of the minivan to slide open the gate.

Kai got the yearbook from the front seat and opened it to a bookmarked page—Edra Monis. He walked towards the house. The woman pulled the vehicle forward into the driveway and was returning to close the gate behind her. He could see two child seats in the rear. A boy of about ten got out of the front passenger seat and headed for the back door in the carport. The woman tugged at the gate. It made a grinding sound. One wheel was off the track.

"Excuse me. Edra Monis?"

She wiped a curl of dark hair from her face and looked at him with the question on her face, *'What now?'* She was in her thirties, and must have been pretty once before she put on a few dozen extra pounds. "Who are you?"

His badge and identification were in his outstretched hand. "Detective Ahuna-Aki, Honolulu Police Department."

The look on her face went to helpless confusion. She glanced back to the open rear door of the Caravan. "Is this about ..." She spoke in a whisper. "... their father? What's he done now?"

He was suddenly interested in what 'their father' could be involved in as a possible tool for leverage. "Is there something you want to tell me—to get your side of the story in?"

"I'm clean. I've passed my piss tests and been to the meetings. I told him not to come back here, so I don't know what crap he's saying. Don't listen to him."

"No, ma'am. This is about something else." He paused to see if she might leap to some other wrong conclusion but she only registered further confusion. "Lana Reynolds."

Her eyes drifted over his left shoulder as if focusing on a distant object moving slowly in the sky. "Lana." She nodded for him to step inside the gate and she pulled at it again.

Kai walked to the far end and lifted the gate so the wheel was on the track. He pushed with her and the gate closed with less screeching.

She unbuckled the second child from the car seat. The girl followed her older brother to the back door. Edra detached the infant carrier from the car seat and grabbed her bag. Several bags of groceries sat on the floor in front of the rear seat. Kai grabbed them and followed her into the carport. The rear door of the Caravan closed automatically.

She led him up four wooden steps into the house. Despite the yellow cabinets and pink Formica countertops, the kitchen was dark. He set the bags of groceries on a small table in the center of the room. She quickly packed the cold items into the refrigerator and left the other items for later. Other things had been left for later—dishes, laundry that needed folding, unopened mail.

The television screamed cartoon dialog from the next room. The boy and the middle child were planted on the floor in the flickering greenish light.

"Do you want something? Diet Coke? Water?"

"No, thanks."

She took a can of Diet Coke from the refrigerator and filled a faded pink plastic tumbler with ice. "Let's go outside. I need a smoke. My mother doesn't let me smoke in here. It's her house."

She picked up a pack of cigarettes and a lighter and looped her arm though the handle of the infant carrier and grabbed the soda and tumbler with her free hand. He followed her to a round patio table behind the carport. She put the infant carrier in a chair, and took another. A tiny fist poked out from under a pink blanket, then retreated. Edra lit up, tilted her head back, and let out a gray jet of smoke from her pursed lips. He gauged the slight breeze to avoid her smoke and took one of the two remaining chairs.

"Lana—after all these years. Why are you asking?"

"This is routine."

"She lived down the street. We went to the same school, right from Kindergarten, all the way up to—" She took another drag. "We were best friends."

He waited, hoping she would add more, but she was staring across the small back yard, over the houses, and towards the mountain ridge.

"Did you stay in touch with her folks after—?"

"*After*? There was no 'after.' She was there and then she wasn't. It wasn't like she died and we knew she was dead. We didn't know. We still don't know. It was like—when I was a kid I had a cat, and she disappeared for a day, and then a second, and a third. The waiting. I couldn't stand it. My mom said it was because she'd gone into heat. I was scared. I felt hurt that she'd left. Abandoned, betrayed—like she'd found another life without me. She came home, hungry and a little beat up, but okay. I kept waiting for Lana to come home—maybe a little scuffed up, but come back to me. She never did, and all I was left with was this anger—the feeling of being betrayed.

"Her folks—it's like they didn't know what to say or do around people. And people didn't know what to say to them. 'Be positive. There's still hope.' I took them casseroles my mom would bake. They had so much fucking food in that house—Mrs. Reynolds had nothing to do all day—she couldn't work, so she made all Lana's favorite foods for when she came back.

"It got so I dreaded going past the house, afraid Mrs. Reynolds might see me and call me up the steps. I didn't think I could hide my anger. It still hurts me." She took a drag and let it out. "I came to hate her. That was it. I hated she was gone and I had to sit at her kitchen table eating bread pudding, her mother watching me, an inch away from crying.

"I wished I could forget Lana—but I couldn't, not really. We'd walked to school together too many times.

Talked about too many stupid boys or slutty girls. Tried too many lipsticks at Long's. Ogled too many *Teen Magazines*. Looked for the perfect jeans too, too, too many times.

"So when they moved away I was happy. I didn't want to know where they went." She stubbed out her third cigarette, and fished around in the pack for a fourth. "But I heard they broke up—her parents. Tough shit for them. I didn't care." She lit the last cigarette.

The two children were standing a few steps to one side.

"What?"

"Mom, we're hungry," the boy said.

"Get the Pizza Rolls from the refrigerator," she said.

The middle child hopped up and down.

She continued her instructions. "Turn the oven to 450. You can do that. I'll be in in a minute." The kids ran back inside. She turned to Kai. "I don't know what else to tell you."

Kai opened the yearbook and pointed to a picture with Lana, Edra, and a third girl with long blonde hair. "Do you know this girl?"

"Angela. Angela Cooper. We met her in high school. She'd have been the class star if it hadn't been for Lana. The last two years of high school she starred in all the school plays. She was *real* popular with the boys. We both were, but I think guys went after her because she was a blond—you know." She shrugged as if it was a given that guys preferred blonds. "She went to college somewhere and got a husband and two kids and a dog. I think she lives in Kapolei. I don't really know. I ran into her at Pearlridge. I was with those two and *hapai* with her," she pointed her cigarette at the infant. "And she had her two, and we were both trying to get our Christmas shopping done. We said we'd get together after the holidays when we weren't so busy. We never did."

"Do you think you still have her number?"

She shook her head but looked through her phone contacts anyway. Her eyebrows went up and she turned the phone to him. He jotted down the number in his notebook.

"Look, I gotta make something for these guys to eat." She stubbed out the cigarette and pushed herself up from the table.

He thanked her and walked through the carport and out the gate. Kapolei—he wasn't driving out there now, not in the middle of rush hour traffic, which was always worse on Fridays.

When he got to his car, he faced the house across the street from the former Reynolds' residence. In the front window a curtain pulled back a few inches. He turned away and opened the door to his car, leaned in, and looked out the opposite side window at the house. The curtain moved. He was being watched.

4

Kai sat in the car for a few minutes. It was hot and stuffy. He still needed an address for Mrs. Reynolds. He called DMV and gave his badge number. He asked for an address for Sara Reynolds. The last address was the one he was sitting at. He climbed out of the car and crossed the street. The name "Yoshimura" was on the mailbox.

The lawn was neatly cut, uniformly green, and weed free. A large part of the yard closest to the house was devoted to a rock and pebble garden. A low stone lantern stood near the path, and a young pine tree, not two-feet tall, stood to one side just beyond. He knocked on the door.

After a few moments, the door opened halfway. A wrinkled, stooped woman leaned towards him, one hand on the doorknob, the other on an aluminum cane. Her skin was powder white, lips pursed and red, hair jet black. She must have been eighty judging by the lines and crags on her face.

"Mrs. Yoshimura?"

Her red lips smiled.

"I'm Detective Kaipupule Ahuna-Aki, with the Honolulu Police Department," he said holding his ID for her to see. "If you have a moment, I'd like to ask you a few questions about your former neighbor." He indicated the house across the street.

Her eyes twinkled and the red lips smiled a touch more. She waved him in with one hand and turned for him to follow.

He kicked off his shoes before stepping inside and closed the door behind him. The front door led directly into the living room. The TV was on but the sound off. The ceiling fan whirred on high, wobble-free, and the fast air was cooling. She stood in front of a straight chair that would leave her feet a few inches off the floor were it not for the pillow placed in front. This is the chair she would have been sitting at to look out the window, only needing to pull back the drapes and inch forward on the chair to see across the street. She indicated the chair across from her, also a prime snooping position.

"May I get you glass of tea?"

He gave a slight bow as consent.

With short steps and the aid of her cane she left the room.

He looked over the living room. The wood floor was dark-stained with a glossy shine. The furniture consisted of four carved straight chairs with sage velvet seat cushions and a matching square coffee table. Against one wall, a small alcove exhibited a long scroll with Chinese characters, and below it, a small vase with a single sprig of small yellow orchid blossoms.

The old lady returned from the kitchen, carrying in one hand a woven cane tray with a picnic basket handle. In the corners, cup holders held glasses and in a larger depression the pitcher. She set it on the coffee table and took her seat, leaning forward to properly serve the tea.

With a spoon she dropped two ice cubes into the glass. She then poured the tea from the pitcher to within an inch of the top, took a straw with a lemon slice loosely around it, and pushed it into the glass. This was not a paper straw, but a slender hollowed cutting of sugar cane. She put a small sprig of mint on top of the floating lemon slice and put the glass on a coaster in front of him. She repeated the process for herself. She then put a small plate of *higashi* confections on the table where they could both reach it, but closer to him. The small pink cookies were molded in the shape of a flower with five overlapping petals, the plumeria.

The palms of his hands were on his thighs and looking down he bowed his head. She was in the same position and likewise bowed—a *shin* bow as best could be accomplished while seated.

He knew he must drink first, and he might have to finish his tea before she'd even start. He took a sip, visibly but subtly indicated he was *tasting* the tea. He commented on the lightness and freshness. She lowered her eyes and smiled, explaining the tea was picked in early spring. He took a napkin and a cookie and finished it in two bites. When he finished his tea, and she'd half finished hers, she sat back in her chair with her feet up on the pillow. Now he could ask his questions.

"Mrs. Yoshimura, I would like to ask you about the Reynolds family that lived across the street."

She nodded her willingness to answer questions.

"Did you know the family well?"

"Oh yes, particularly the girl, Lana. You have come to ask about her, since she cannot be found." She said it as if her disappearance were a recent event.

"The family moved. Do you know where they live

now?"

"Yes. Once get Christmas card—from Sara Reynolds, the mother. I will get for you before you go," she said as if she assumed more questions would follow.

This woman sits by her window everyday observing the street. She'd be a reservoir of good information, but probably also trades information—if she finds out something she will pass it on to others in her network. "What can you tell me about the family?"

She leaned her head slightly to one side. "Russell, good looking *haole* boy. Tall and strong, the skinny-kind, not big-muscle kind. Hard work man. I see him come home very tired, sun burned face and arms, dirty shirt, dirty pants, boots."

"Did he work construction?"

"Construction, yes. Roads too, but still have time to play with his children."

"Children? How many?"

"Boy first, then a girl. Chris and Lana. They had a dog, too."

"And the mother?"

"Sara. *Hapa* girl, very pretty. Dance hula, she." The old woman mimed the swaying of a dancer. "Her mother *nissei*, father Big Island Hawaiian. Sara worked at home, she sew dresses, skirts, blouses. She good eye, good hands. Very creative. See one kimono and make dress *hopi* style, then blouse, then jacket—all from one look at kimono. Her clothes were at old Liberty House at Kāhala Mall. You remember Liberty House?"

"Yes. Where is the family now?"

She smiled as if to say 'you impatient boy.' She would tell him at her own pace. "After Lana go missing, Sara too sad, stop working. Husband I don't see so much—I think he become drunken man. In one year, they move out. They get divorce. I never see again."

She got up from her chair, and with the aid of her cane, took a few short steps to a cabinet. She removed a small box and returned to her chair setting the box on the table. She opened the box and slid an envelope from the front. Without letting it go she showed it to him.

Sara Iwamoto, with a Mānoa address.

"She took her mother's maiden name after divorce."

The box was stuffed with photographs. The one on top was of Mrs. Yoshimura with Lana.

"May I?"

She nodded her consent.

He removed the top photo. A teenage Lana had her arms around the old lady. The next photo they were in the front garden, Lana on her knees, her hands in the soil. The next showed them cutting *mochi* into squares, another of them in the kitchen, and yet another of Lana in a summer kimono in *shin* bow. This woman was more than a neighbor. She was a surrogate grandmother.

He looked at a close-up of Lana. It was not a smile that he saw, but a look of being happy. Why did that surprise him? Because at her age he was anything but happy? He'd have loved to have known her when they were both fifteen. Maybe some of her happiness would have rubbed off on him. Maybe he'd be happy today—as if this girl he didn't know would still be in his life.

"You can keep this picture," the old woman said. What had she seen in his face to make such a gesture? Every one of these was a prized possession for her.

He lowered his eyes in unworthy thanks.

The old lady tried to smile. "You come and ask questions. It mean only one thing. You have found her."

She looked out the window. "And she is dead."

There was no network of gossips. She sat each day in the chair by the window to watch for Lana to come home. What had he just taken away from this old lady? He reached to take her frail hand in his, but she pulled her hand away. Without looking, she bowed and shooed him off.

He returned her bow, rose from his chair, and silently left the house. He put his shoes on at the front steps and walked over to his car, and drove slowly, respectfully, out of the neighborhood.

He redialed DMV. As of eight years ago, Sara Iwamoto had a new address. He changed course.

5

Mature trees shaded Kāhala Avenue. This older part of the street had no sidewalks and parking was not allowed on the verges. Thick hedges or rock walls with gates obscured most of the homes on this side of the street. The lots were wide and, although it couldn't be seen from the street, they stretched down to a sandy beach. The homes were large and reminiscent of old Hawai'i style, with double-pitch roofs and stucco over thick masonry walls. He'd been in houses like these or seen them in the home magazines. The rooms had rooms—bedrooms large enough to include a sitting area with a sofa and side chairs, and to one side a dressing room attached to a walk-in closet. The kitchen would have a pantry larger than his apartment. Not that he would choose to live here.

He found the address and parked on the grass in front of the moss rock wall. He got out of the car. Just to the left, a roadside sign stated 'Vote Osterlick for City Prosecutor.' It was neatly placed. The mailbox sat on a small pillar of stone at the edge of the road. He would have opened it to check for the names of the occupants but it was locked. A brass plate said 'Osterlick' in script. So this was the home of the great Martin Osterlick, Esquire—attorney to the rich and famous, and usually guilty? Sara had certainly moved up after her first marriage.

The gate to the driveway was open. It was meant to operate automatically via remote, but the gate had a serious bend at one end as if a driver hadn't waited for it to open fully before attempting to drive through.

He pressed a call button on the intercom at the entrance—no response. He stepped through the opening and walked up the drive towards the house. The front yard was large with a collection of whicker lawn furniture more complete than his living room set. Dense landscaping along the rock walls to either side blocked the view of neighboring houses creating a tropical oasis. This is how nature would be if God could afford it.

He walked up the smooth drive to the front door. Coral stone, a porous light-colored rock, paved the walk to the broad, shaded porch. He knocked on the front door and waited. He looked for a buzzer or doorbell, but if someone got this far the security cameras would have already spotted them. No one came to the door. He couldn't imagine a house this size without help—a maid, housekeeper, groundskeeper?

He followed a path to the side of the house. From here he could see a portion of the rear yard with more lawn furniture, this time chaise lounges, and the ocean beyond. As he rounded the corner, he saw what every exclusive house on the beach must have—its own swimming pool, set in a patio of Terrazzo marble—because it's not enough to just have something, it's about having something in ostentatious redundancy.

Nobody was home. He walked back the way he came and crossed in front of the house. Beyond the front entrance the paved driveway led to a garage with four stout wooden doors suggesting a carriage house. One of the doors was open. He looked inside. This parking bay was empty, and so was the one next to it. Beyond that he could see a black Porsche Carrera Whale Fin and a silver Lexus SUV. On the walls were the toys that came with affluence. Several pairs of skis, a snowboard, and a high performance, carbon fiber triathlon bike hung from its front wheel. The bike alone had to be worth a couple grand.

"Who are you?"

He turned to see a girl in a Saint Teresa's uniform, white blouse over navy pleated skirt, her hands in fists on her hips, her feet planted on a skate board, her eyes boring into his.

"What are you doing here?" she demanded.

He looked at her but couldn't say anything. His eyes and his brain and his mouth were caught in some kind of paradox. He focused on her face, not quite believing what he saw. Finally he said something, but it made no sense even as he heard himself speak.

"Lana?"

6

"The question, asshole, is who are you?" She said it with plenty of confidence as she stepped off the skateboard, tipped the front end up, and grabbed it by the nose.

He pulled out his identification and held it out for her to see. "Detective Kaipupule Ahuna-Aki, Honolulu Police Department." He stared at her. Dark, sun-streaked hair fell in loose waves framing her face—the same face he'd looked at in the photographs—the same eyes, the same nose, the same lips—except this girl wasn't smiling. Not even close. "I'm looking for Sara Iwamoto."

"And this is about?"

"This is about—" he almost said 'you,' but this girl was not Lana Reynolds. "This is about— "

"Lana. Something to do with her. She's my sister, if you haven't figured it out by now, detective."

Of course this was her sister. The resemblance was too great. If this girl only smiled they'd be identical.

"That must mean you've found her." She lowered her head and softened her voice. "I don't suppose she was smoking black tar in a brothel in Cambodia. She's dead isn't she?"

He didn't respond but knew she was reading his face for the answer.

"That's the last requirement for sainthood." She walked toward the front door and said over her shoulder, "You might as well wait inside."

He followed her onto the front porch. "What's your name?"

She turned and faced him square on. "Don't you want to keep calling me Lana?"

He shook his head. "Who are you?"

She looked him over slowly as if trying to figure him out. Or maybe she was about to throw a punch. "Nobody wants to know who I am. Not even the shrink who listens to my made up fantasies three times a week."

He took a step closer, within arm's reach, and it surprised her. "What's your name?"

"Ka'ena," she said almost apologetically. She stared into his eyes as if there was something significant she could learn about him.

He wouldn't look away, or fake a non-threatening smile, or look shocked by her behavior.

"My name is Ka'ena," she repeated with a strong voice.

She pushed open the door and kicked her shoes off in the entry hall. He slipped off his shoes and closed the door behind him.

The ground floor plan was wide open. Straight ahead five French doors framed a view of a covered lanai, the patio and pool, an expanse of lawn, and the Pacific Ocean. Ahead to the right was the living room with a large fireplace at the far end. To the left was the dining room and beyond, facing the patio, was the kitchen. Ka'ena pulled open one door of a very large stainless steel refrigerator. She held a small container of yogurt. "Do you want anything? Beer? Soda?"

"I'm fine. When does your mother get home?"

She shrugged. "You can never tell." She peeled off the lid and licked the trace of pink from the foil.

He sat on a stool on one side of the kitchen island, and she leaned on the counter on the other side. She dipped her finger in the container then stuck it in her mouth.

"A big house like this. No maid? No housekeeper?"

"Mother probably fired them all. She does that every now and then. She decides she's going to be a better housewife and do all the chores herself, and tells them to go home. But then Mother quickly realizes she's such a basket case she can't do a fucking thing, and so she self-medicates with Tanqueray."

He thought about the bent gate at the driveway.

"It's okay. My stepdad will hire them back tomorrow with a little extra for the inconvenience. They look forward to the extra time off every few weeks and hope she does it early so they get the whole day off." She finished the yogurt and tossed the container in the trash. She went to the refrigerator and removed three limes. She carried them to a cutting board and cut them into wedges. She trimmed the center, removed the seeds, and put the wedges into a bowl.

"You go to Saint Teresa's?"

"Yeah. I'm a freshman."

"Have you been to the library?"

"Why would I go to the library? Why would anybody? I can get more information on my phone in a minute than I could find in the library in a week. The library is for total losers." She stiffened. "Is there something in the library? Don't tell me—a shrine where I'm supposed to pay homage."

"No, just someone who remembers your sister."

"Well, they'll be disappointed when they meet me." She stared at the ocean.

Just then there was a rapid beeping sound. A flat screen monitor under a kitchen cabinet showed a head-on view of the front gate. A car was coming in, not quite making it through the narrow opening.

"What the f — ?" She quickly headed for the front door. "It's Mother."

He followed her and stepped into his shoes. They stood on the front porch as a midnight blue Jaguar XJ pulled up the drive. It stopped abruptly a few feet short of the garage door. The passenger side of the Jag was scraped the entire length and when he walked around to the driver's side he saw a scrape along the rear quarter.

The door opened and Sara Iwamoto swung her legs out of the car. She stood with some difficulty. She was a fiftyish version of Ka'ena and Lana, a little taller, a little heavier, and with a few lines at the corners of the mouth and the edges of her eyes. Her hair was styled, and the clothes were expensive, but a little out of date. She was still a strikingly beautiful woman.

"Hello, Ms. Iwamoto. I'm Detective— "

She put a hand up to stop him. "Please, please, just wait a moment. I've had a bad day and I need to sit down." She pushed the car door but didn't manage to get it closed. She walked to the front entrance and as she approached Ka'ena, she said, "How's my girl?" But she kept walking without waiting for an answer. She kicked her high heels off as she crossed the entry hall. She dropped her bag on the way to the living room and let herself collapse into a leather easy chair facing the empty fireplace.

"I've had such a crappy day," she said, presumably to Ka'ena who followed her into the living room but stayed a few feet back. "So much noise—the vacuum cleaner, leaf blowers. I couldn't stand it. Then I went to the club to meet the girls. I was waiting at the bar and wondering where they were. I asked that young bartender why they could be so late. He said I was the one who was late—they met yesterday. When did they change it to Wednesday? He said yesterday was Thursday. I said, no, that couldn't be."

"You slept all day yesterday," Ka'ena said.

"What?"

"You were still in bed when I got home."

"No, I—"

"I brought you a bowl of soup and some crackers, and you ate it in bed."

She was slowly shaking her head.

"You asked me how school was," Ka'ena prompted. "I sat on the bed and we talked."

Sara looked past her as if something was written on the wall but was just too far to read. "And—what did you say?"

"I told you—" Ka'ena looked away so Kai couldn't see the hurt in her face. Her voice hardened. "I told you I was raped by a gang of bull dykes, and when I reported it to the nuns they made me repeat the story while they masturbated."

"Why do you say things like that?" She squeezed her eyes shut and rubbed her temples. "It makes my headache worse."

Ka'ena looked caught between defiant and apologetic. She shifted from foot to foot.

"Will you get me something?"

Without waiting for further instruction, Ka'ena went to the kitchen and put several ice cubes into a tall glass. She poured a few fingers from the distinctive Tanqueray bottle and filled the glass the rest of the way with tonic water. She squeezed a lime wedge on top and stirred lightly with a straw. Ka'ena brought the drink to the living room and placed a coaster on the left arm of her mother's chair before she set it down. She held the glass until Sara put her hand around it, but even in this exchange, the two never touched.

Sara took a sip. "Thank you, thank you."

"Mom." Ka'ena nodded towards Kai.

She turned his way and looked as if she were seeing him for the first time. "Who are you?"

"Detective Kaipupule Ahuna-Aki, Honolulu Police Department," he said stepping in front of her chair.

"You probably want my husband. He's not home."

"What I have to say concerns you." He waited for her to focus her attention on him. "This morning, skeletal remains of a young woman were uncovered in Ewa."

Sara froze, the drink in her hand a few inches from her lips. She looked through Kai as if he were transparent.

Ka'ena took the glass from her hand.

"We believe them to be your daughter. The Medical Examiner will verify this by comparing the remains with dental records. We need your consent to access that information. But everything right now indicates it's Lana." He unfolded the release form and placed it on the arm of her chair with his pen.

"How? I mean— " She absently took the pen.

"The rail line. They were digging the footings for one of the supports." He pointed to a line on the form and watched her scrawl a signature.

"What does this mean?"

"We'll have to wait to see what the Medical Examiner finds. If it gives us something to work with then an investigation will be opened up. But often, after this many years, even with the remains, there may not be anything new to go on."

"Remains." She sighed.

He'd made the notification and had the release. He was free to go now. It was not yet end of shift, but he could call it a day. By the time he drove back to the station house the shift would be over.

"Those are the remains? Then what am I?" Her eyes beseeched his. "I lost my daughter, I lost my husband, I lost everything I loved. My entire life—gone. I was a refugee, moving about in a fog, surrounded by destruction, with nothing left from before. Everything gone. I'm the remains, like an unbroken tea pot in a landscape of rubble."

He wanted to leave. He'd done death notifications before, telling mothers their child had died in a car accident, or a loved one in a violent crime. He was always able to shake it off and stay detached. Somehow this one was different. He didn't know if it was the girl—the girls—the one he'd wished he'd known growing up or the one that was here now, or the mother, a barely functional alcoholic. He just wanted to get out of there.

"What do I do now?"

"When the Medical Examiner has completed their report you'll be contacted about mortuary arrangements. If there will be an investigation, we'll let you know."

"Oh, please no," she whispered. She looked up at him pleading. "I don't want another investigation. I couldn't go through it again."

More than likely there would be no investigation. Even if there were, he would be the last person they would assign to it. "It's not my call, Ms. Iwamoto." He took a business card from his wallet and put Lieutenant Coelho's number on the back. "Here's how you can contact me or my supervisor." He placed the card on the coffee table. "I'm sorry for your loss."

He walked to the entry and slipped on his shoes. He was out the door and off the porch but he could hear the girl running behind him.

"That's it?" Ka'ena grabbed his arm to stop him. "I'm sorry for your loss?"

He pulled away and continued up the driveway to the street.

"Aren't you going to try to find out who did this?" She was in front of him, walking backwards. She pushed on his chest, arms out straight.

"I'm sorry. There's nothing I can do."

She was barefoot and didn't have the traction to slow him down. He opened his car door. When he saw the panic in her face, he wanted to tell her to run away from home, get out of this toxic situation, change your name, forget there was ever a perfect, beautiful sister who looked just like you—but isn't you. He got in the car.

"You're just going to leave?"

He shut the door and started the engine. She was holding the door handle. He started off slow, hoping she'd let go. She ran alongside saying something he couldn't quite make out.

"You're just going to leave me here?"

7

Kai drove to Diamond Head Lookout and parked. It was nearly five. His call to Lieutenant Coelho went to voice mail. He left a message stating he'd made the notification to Sara Reynolds, now Sara Iwamoto, and emailed a report to the office.

    He got out of his SUV and looked down at the sea and the surfers hoping to catch a wave. The break was clean — no wind. Set after set rolled in clean and strong from the south. It was late summer here, so a late winter storm somewhere in the southern hemisphere was sending this swell. The lineup of surfers was long. Every so often a larger wave would begin to break 50 yards further out than the others and none of the surfers were in position to catch it. He had his board in the SUV, something a cop with a subsidized vehicle wouldn't be allowed to do. He wanted to get in the ocean quick. After that family he needed to get clean.

    He got the board and a small backpack with his towel and board shorts out of the SUV. The path to the rocky beach was steep, but so well worn and familiar he was down in a minute. He wrapped the towel around his waist and changed into his board shorts. He folded his clothes and the towel and put them into the backpack and stowed it against a large rock where it was in sight from the water.

He waded into the shorebreak, splashed some water on the board, and took a handful of water to bless himself. This last motion was more out of tradition then religious sentiment. He paddled out wide around any surfers riding in and got to the back of the lineup. He nodded to those he knew, and even to those he didn't who looked like they knew him. He stayed way back and saw several good waves with surfers jumping up and catching a ride.

After a few minutes the wave came. He turned the board towards the shore. The water swelled up behind him tipping the nose down. He stretched out on the deck and paddled hard a few strokes. He was moving faster than his paddling could propel him. He pushed up and was quickly on his feet in a low crouch.

The board sped down the face of the wave as if sliding down a hill of marbles. He threaded through the other surfers who were too late to catch this wave. As he descended the wall of water, it rose behind him and became steeper, intent to lean over him. He cut to the left across the face of the ascending water. A shimmering curtain of green dropped before him and he was in the tube. Just beyond the nose of his board, through a moving green oval, was the only blue sky he could see. The tight end of this blue-green tunnel was catching up to him, squeezing the tail of his board. The oval of upward-rushing water slowly tipped its axis. It would soon catch him and suck him up and over and down—but it hadn't yet.

And as that green enclosure tightened around him a gust of spray blew past him and suddenly he was out and into the blue. He stood erect on his board, arms stretched out. He could hear the whistles and cheers from those in the line up behind him. His arms were out like in a crucifixion scene. At that moment he felt he'd come to death and was reborn another human with great new possibilities.

On shore, someone had climbed up on the rock and was looking in his backpack. He dropped onto his board to paddle the rest of the way in and navigated the rocks. He slid off the board and carried it pinched under his arm and made his way to his gear. Sitting on the rock Indian style was a girl in a white bikini. Ka'ena.

"That was a pretty slick ride. Pretty slick. You related to the great Kilauea Aki?"

How'd she know about him? He'd died before she was born. The legend persists. "Aki's a common name. What are you doing here?"

"I saw your car up top. The board wasn't in it so I thought … "

"So you thought you'd come down and look through my stuff." Sitting on the rock put her at eye level. He looked away from her. The salt water and the low angle of the sun stung his eyes. He wiped them. She was still there.

She shrugged.

He put his board down and climbed up next to her. He took the bag. "I'm not going to be able to do what you want."

"Are you sure you know what I want?" When she turned to him her knee brushed his thigh.

"You want me to work on the case and solve your sister's murder. They gave me the rest of the day to wrap it up. It's after five. That's it. No more."

"Okay. But today's not over. There's about six and a half hours left—that's almost a full shift."

"The case is fifteen years old. I don't have the case file. I can't even get it without my lieutenant's approval."

"What if it had been *me* that was murdered?"

He shook his head.

"And they threw shovelfuls of dirt on me, covering my body, my face."

He stared out to sea so he wouldn't have the image of her being buried in his mind.

"Maybe I'm not even dead. They just think I'm dead. As the dirt gets deeper it gets harder to breathe. Dirt's in my nose, my throat, but somehow I'm hoping somebody will come to rescue me."

God, it could have been her. She looked so much like her they could be the same person. But they weren't. Today her sister would be thirty—his own age.

"I'm suffocating. Don't let me die. I need help."

"No." But he knew he could. He knew how. And she desperately needed rescuing.

"Will you just let me suffocate? Day by day, shovelful by shovelful. Help me. I need you."

"If it were you …"

"What would you do?"

"Look at the people around you."

"Who?"

"Start with your parents. Find out if someone had anything to gain—insurance, trust fund. Find out who your friends were, boyfriends, girlfriends, frenemies. Start close and widen the circle."

"Okay, then let's get going. You've talked to my mother. My dad and my brother, they're out of the picture."

"No. Start with them."

"My father—my real father—he went to the mainland after the divorce. I've never met him."

He knew what that was like. He was fourteen when he met his father for the first time. "What about your brother?"

"Chris. He was eighteen years old when I was born. I can barely remember him. He came home a few times on leave. He was in the Army. He died in Iraq."

Two possible sources of information gone. Sara might be next to useless. How reliable could she be if she couldn't remember what happened yesterday?

"Let's find out who her friends were," she said.

He already knew who they were. That information was in his notebook in the car. "Why is this so important to you? You didn't know her. Her existence has only made your life miserable."

"She and I are nearly identical, practically the same DNA. Everybody says I look like her. They want me to act like her, to be her."

"Just be yourself."

"That doesn't work. It scares the hell out of them. It scares me sometimes. I won't be free of her until I find out who she really was. Maybe when I find out how she died I'll know. The violent dreams I have—are they about me or are they about her?"

He shivered from the water evaporating on his skin. He got his backpack and stood behind the rock. He wrapped the towel around his waist and dressed.

She watched, then slid off the rock. She put on a t-shirt and cut-off jeans, then reached into the waistband, untied the strings of her bikini bottom, and pulled them out one leg opening of her cut-offs. She dusted sand off her feet and stepped into a beat-up pair of Vans. She grabbed her skateboard and started the climb up.

Kai slung the backpack over one shoulder, put the board under one arm, and followed her up the trail. She had long legs and he could see the muscles working—all that skateboarding. The cutoffs were short, and showed a little cheek. Her hips swayed as she climbed up the hill and the shorts tightened around her butt in interesting ways. He looked up and saw she'd looked over her shoulder at him. She smiled—well, almost.

At the top he stowed the board on the Outback's roof rack. He combed back his wet hair with his fingers. He looked a little crumpled, but it was good enough.

"So what's first?" Ke'ana asked.

"I want to talk to the boyfriend."

"She had a boyfriend?"

"Yeah. Zack something." He reached into the driver's side door and retrieved his notebook. He found the notation. "Zachary Pizzo. Maybe he's still around. If he's got a driver's license I can get an address from DMV."

"Great. Let's go." She tried to open the passenger side door but it was locked. "Hey, open up."

"I didn't say anything about you coming along."

"I've got to go."

"I can't take you on an official police investigation."

"I thought you got off duty at five?"

"You can't have it both ways, little girl. If I'm working the case, I'm working."

She looked across the roof of the car. Those eyes—the panic he'd seen as she ran beside his car, as she suffocated in that house, as the red dirt covered her face. He unlocked the passenger side door and she opened it. "I'll work it until nine. That's it." He could still make it to Anna's and meet up with the blond anthropologist.

Ka'ena slid into the front passenger seat. "Why not go until midnight? That would *double* your time—get twice as much done."

"I can't be knocking on doors until midnight, not even until nine. People go to bed Besides ... "

"You got some place to go? Hot date?"

He was ready for something to go right this day but didn't want to discuss his potential social life. "Besides, you must have a curfew. A time you need to be home by."

"It's not a school night. I can stay out as late as I want."

"I doubt that. Don't you think you should call your mother and clear it with her?"

"Fine." She pulled a phone from her back pocket and touched an icon of her mother. "Mom, I'm with Detective Ahuna-Aki ... I told him I want to help with the investigation ... it's just asking people questions and things ... but I want to stay out until midnight ..."

"Nine o'clock," Kai said.

"Ten? Okay, ten o'clock. Thanks, mom." She ended the call. "She said I could stay out until ten."

"I'd've liked to have heard it from her."

"Huh? Oh, yeah. You want me to call her back so you can talk to her?"

He didn't want anything to do with that woman. "Nah, that's okay." If he got her home by ten he could still make it to Anna's by ten thirty.

He called DMV and got the address for Zachary Pizzo—no stops, no wants, no warrants. Zack did have a history of citations for a modified vehicle. Typically that meant driving a chopped car—a low rider or a monster truck.

"So what's our first stop?"

"Zack lives a block from where your mother lived fifteen years ago. My guess is he never left the old neighborhood." The sun set as they drove to Kaimuki. They pulled up to a neat single-wall house on a small lot. "The way this is going to work is, you wait in the car and I'll go in and speak to him."

"I don't think so. I'll go in with you. I may have questions of my own to ask."

"Like what?"

"Like were he and Lana doin' it?"

That would be an important piece of information and would show the level of their involvement, if the interviewee answered truthfully. "I'm not leading with that question. We need to come up on it slowly."

"You said we."

"I meant me. Wait here." He got out of the car and walked around the front.

She opened the door and stepped out. "I'm just stretching my legs."

He walked up the pathway to the house. He glanced over his shoulder—she was leaning against the car. He climbed the steps and knocked on the wall next to the door. A gray haired woman came to the entry. She wore a faded housedress. "Yes?"

Kai held up his badge. "I'm Detective Kaipupule Ahuna-Aki, Honolulu Police Department. I'd like to speak with Zachary Pizzo. Is he at home?"

"No, he works until six—later sometimes. But Fridays he hangs out with the guys."

"Where does he work?"

"SVT Auto Body, on Queen Street. I'm his mother. What's this about?"

"This is a routine investigation."

She was looking over Kai's shoulder. "That girl—she looks like ... " She squinted her eyes, then pulled up a pair of glasses that hung from a string around her neck. "Is this about Lana?"

"Yes, Mrs. Pizzo. I'd like to ask you some questions, if you don't mind."

"Oh, I don't know. I don't think I have anything to say."

"It will only take a few minutes of your time."

She slowly shook her head, her gaze still fixed past him. He sensed Ka'ena approach from behind.

"You look just like her."

Ka'ena stood next to Kai.

"She even wore cutoffs." Mrs. Pizzo's eyes roamed over the girl, resting on the inch or two of the jeans front pockets hanging below the ragged hem. "But maybe not so short. Who are you?"

"Ka'ena Reynolds. Lana's sister."

"Now I remember. Sara was pregnant when she left."

"Can we come in, Mrs. Pizzo?" Ka'ena asked.

The woman pushed open the screen door and led them to the kitchen table.

8

"Have a seat. I've got some coffee, detective, if you like."

"Thank you, Mrs. Pizzo," Kai said.

She placed a mug in front of Kai and poured from an old aluminum coffee pot. She reached into the refrigerator and pulled out a bottle of soda. "And I've got Sprite."

"I'd prefer coffee," Ka'ena said.

"Since when do you— " Mrs. Pizzo caught herself.

"Lana drank Sprite, didn't she?"

Mrs. Pizzo nodded. "Yes, she did, my dear. She'd sit right where you're sitting and drink Sprite from a glass with ice."

"That's something about her I didn't know," Ka'ena said. "Something she liked."

"And your mother's bread pudding," Kai said. "At least that's what I've heard."

"Oh yes, your mother makes the best bread pudding."

Ka'ena slowly shook her head. She didn't say a word but Kai could see it on her face— I've never had it. She's never made it for me.

Mrs. Pizzo put a mug in front of Ka'ena and filled it with coffee, then poured some in her own cup, which was already on the table.

"Mrs. Pizzo," Kai said. "What can you tell us about Zack and Lana?"

"Oh, they knew each other since elementary school. Walked home together every day, along with another girl who lived up the street from Lana."

"Edra."

"Yes, Edra. You know, that's how I knew something had happened. I mean some people said she ran off to Hollywood or some such thing, but not Lana. She was loyal to her friends. They were friends for life."

"Lana and Zack. How close were they?"

"Well, they did a lot of stuff together—mostly with the theater. They were a good team. She was the creative type, always with wild ideas. She got that from her mom, the clothing designer. Zack was the guy who could do things, get broken things to work, make sets and backdrops, get props, run the lighting and the sound. He's a wiz with tools, even to this day. He went to community college, over on Dillingham, got his AA and learned how to do auto body repair. He was already good with the paints. He had a summer job and saved up for a sprayer."

"Besides working on theater, did they do things together? Go on dates?"

"They were together all the time. Go on a date? Well, they went to the movies a lot. But they'd been doing that for years. If what you mean is did he ever kiss her? I think he did, but I don't know that for sure. I doubt it ever got beyond that—she was a good girl, you know."

"So I've heard," Ka'ena said softly.

"Mrs. Pizzo, do you know if any other boys took Lana out on dates? Any of the actors in the plays?"

She shrugged. "I don't know. That's a question for her mother—for your mother." She looked at Ka'ena. "Can't she tell you anything?"

Ka'ena seemed unable to find the right words to answer Mrs. Pizzo.

"We wanted to get your impression," Kai said.

"I don't think there was anyone serious—I'd have heard about it, or at least felt it, from Zack. Although come to think of it, the last summer—well, I don't know."

"What happened the last summer?"

"Zack has sort of a slight build. He's always been skinny. That last summer, he got a set of dumbbells and started working out in the carport. Maybe it's just a phase boys go through—their self image. But I remember wondering if they'd gone to the beach and, you know, sort of noticed how developed she was and how undeveloped he was. Or maybe she was looking at other boys. Whatever it was, he spent a lot of time working out—not that it did a thing. He was still just as skinny as a rod. But it did make me think of Tony. He was a little more filled out."

"Tony?"

"From West Side Story. The boy who played that part was, you know, more developed. And he got to kiss Lana."

"So Zack could have been jealous?"

Mrs. Pizzo almost answered, then held back. "I don't know if I'm going to say anything like that." She looked at Kai suspiciously. "In fact, maybe I better not say anything else."

He'd pushed it too far and she shut down. He tried a less threatening question, "Where does he hang out after work?"

"I don't seem to remember the name of the place."

"Thank you for your help, and for the coffee." Kai got up to leave and Ka'ena followed. Kai walked to the front door, taking a good look at the living room as he passed. A leatherette recliner faced the TV, and to its right a side table with the remote sitting on top of several car magazines—the kind with a girl in a bikini and high heels standing in front of a tricked out Mitsubishi Evo. The couch had extra pillows and a shawl where Mrs. Pizzo sat. They were the only inhabitants of the house—no Mr. Pizzo, no siblings, no girlfriend.

He crossed the front yard with Ka'ena right behind him. When he opened the car door he looked over the roof. Mrs. Pizzo was watching him, her hands on her hips guarding her home.

"She'll call her son. Tell him we're asking questions," he said when he was fastening his seat belt.

"You think he did it? You think he got jealous and—"

"No, he was fifteen. He didn't have access to a backhoe to bury her, or a car to transport the body."

"But he knows about cars and machinery. Maybe he knew how to use a backhoe, or could figure it out."

"Let's talk to him before jumping to conclusions. But we've got a stop to make before we look for Zack." Kai started the car and drove off. He checked Sara Reynolds's address before she moved to Kāhala.

They were a mile or two from the original Reynolds house. "I know where we are," Ka'ena said as they pulled to the curb in a residential neighborhood. "Are you sure this is where you want to go?"

This was an older part of Mānoa and the houses were predominantly a Bungalow style that was popular seventy years ago and was in great demand again for the charm of the architecture and the proximity to the university. The lots were bigger than the Reynolds's property with deeper front yards, and all the houses had well tended lawns. The neighborhood was still middle class, but Kai remembered the nuances within the classes when he was in high school. Some kids had nicer clothes and their parents drove new cars. Some had cars of their own and threw parties that included all the popular girls. "You know this house? Who lives here?"

"Grandma Osterlick. My stepdad's mother."

9

"Your mother lived here before your Kāhala home."

"Yeah, when I was little."

Kai was looking for connections to Lana. Her brother was dead, her father was in the wind, her mother was a drunk. "I need to know more about what was going on fifteen years ago. Maybe Mrs. Osterlick can tell me things your mother might not remember."

"I doubt it," Ka'ena said. "She's a crabby old bitch and a little, you know, crazy. We should just go talk to that guy Zack."

"We will. But that's over in Kaka'ako and we'll have to look for his hangout. We're here now. We might as well spend ten minutes talking to her."

"Go right ahead."

"Why don't you come with me?"

"Oh, this'll be fun."

They stepped up on the porch. A dog yipped behind the door. Someone stirred inside. "Who is it, Rosco? Who's at the door?"

A small scraggly-haired dog ran out and nipped at their ankles. A short, thin, bent old woman stood in the doorway and looked at them. Her steel gray hair contrasted with her black dress. She squinted through wire-rimmed glasses and after a moment acknowledged Ka'ena. "You? Humph, what do you want?" And she turned to Kai. "And who are you?"

"I'm Detective Kaipupule Ahuna-Aki, Honolulu Police Department."

"Police? What has she done this time?" She shook her head and looked ready to spit on Ka'ena. "Just put her in jail. That's where she's headed, the good for nothing whore."

"Hello, Grandmother Osterlick," Ka'ena said. "Back from your broom ride early?" She stomped a foot and the dog ran behind the old lady.

"She has no respect for anyone. She is part evil, I swear."

"That's me. Spawn of the devil."

The old lady looked at Kai. "What is it you want?"

"Mrs. Osterlick, I'd like to talk to you about when Sara Reynolds came to live with you."

"Sara didn't live with me. She lived in the *'ohana* unit in the back. She had this illegitimate child after she'd divorced her husband." She shook her head. "And my boy felt sorry for her and let her live in the back. But then she twisted Martin around her little finger and the next thing you know he wanted to marry her. I knew there would be trouble when Martin first laid eyes on you." The old lady pointed a crooked finger at Ka'ena. "I saw you at school and I knew he was smitten with you."

"With me?"

"He didn't dare talk to you. You were always with those other boys, the rough boys, the dirty boys. The ones whose fathers went off to dirty, sweaty jobs and whose mothers worked jobs that required no education—check-out at Long's, vacuuming hotel lobby floors, sewing other people's clothes. Humph. I don't know what my Martin saw in you. Your type is cheap and easy and often gets in trouble. I told him he could do better. Much better than you."

"Me?"

"I think you're confusing her with Sara."

"Sara. You," and spittle flew towards Ka'ena. "One of those dirty children."

"You're the one that's dirty, you old dried-up, spider-infested, skunky-smelling cunt. Fuck you, and your little turd-eating dog too." Ka'ena marched back to the car.

"You see? You see? That's the kind of evil person she is."

"I'm sorry to have disturbed you," Kai said. "I'll see that she goes straight to jail. We have to watch that kind of girl."

The old lady looked at Kai, then gave him an appreciative nod.

"I'm wondering if I could stop by at another time and talk to you about when she was here, perhaps look at the *'ohana* unit.

"It's been locked up ever since."

"Maybe she left something."

"You mean evidence? Here?

"It might help us put her away."

Her eyes narrowed to slits. "And put her away once and for all?"

"Yes, I'll put her away once and for all." He gave her his card. "When I come back you can show me the *'ohana* unit."

"Certainly, detective. I'll look forward to helping you put that little whore where she belongs." She closed the door.

Kai returned to the car and got in. The girl yanked the seat belt repeatedly, but it wouldn't unspool. She gave up.

He headed for Kaka'ako to look for Zack. "Not your favorite relative."

"We're *not* related."

"One thing maybe you could help me with. She said, 'What's she done this time?' What did she mean by that?"

"She had me mixed up with my mother or with Lana. You saw that."

"Sure she was mixed up, but she never knew Lana."

"My mother went to the same high school as my stepfather."

"And your mother got into trouble when she was young?"

"How should I know?"

"Or maybe she was talking about some trouble you got into?"

She was quiet.

He waited her out.

"So what? It was no big deal."

"How big?"

"Not that big."

"Did anyone get killed?"

"No. One guy got stabbed, that's all, but he was out of the hospital in a week. Not even."

"How many guys were there?"

"Two. The other one just had cuts to his hands."

"Tell me about it."

"I was riding with these two boys. They got into a fight. One had a knife."

"Riding? Was the car stolen?"

"He would have taken it back if we hadn't crashed."

"And the fight. Let me guess. It was over you."

"Yeah, so?"

"And these boys—how old were they?"

"One was nineteen. The other a little older."

He waited.

"Twenty-three."

"And you got arrested?"

"Yeah. They're doing time. But they squelched mine."

"You mean they sealed your record. They do that for juveniles."

"No, they squelched it. Erased. Deleted. Zapped. My stepfather's got some kind of pull."

Kai nodded. That's right, he's Martin Osterlick. "How did he do that?"

"He got the other two to plead it out."

"He represented them too?" He already knew the answer was yes. It had to be some kind of conflict of interest. And the arrest report got altered somehow, and gratuities extended to the arresting officers. Still, there must have been some consequences for the girl. "So that's why you see a shrink three times a week."

Her tone said *'well, isn't it obvious?'* "Rich parents do that sort of thing when they have a sexually active fourteen-year old who dreams about violent death." She shrugged her shoulders as if to say *'so there.'*

They were nearing Kaka'ako. Kai activated the GPS on his phone. "Directions to SVT Fender Shop."

A female voice came back, "SVT Auto Body Repair, Queen Street. Take Ward Avenue current direction two blocks. Turn right on Queen Street. Take Queen Street one and one half blocks to SVT Auto Body Repair, on the right. Estimated time one minute."

Kai turned onto Queen Street and pulled up in front of a closed metal garage door. The place was dark as were all the surrounding businesses. Kaka'ako was an area of more than a dozen auto body repair shops and auto mechanics, auto supply stores, windshield glass, detailing, and other auto related small businesses. The streets were narrow and without sidewalks. Often the businesses appropriated part of the roadway as their own customer parking, or to simply store a car until it was ready for pick up, further tightening the streets.

Kai used the GPS to locate bars within a half-mile radius. He eliminated the bars *ma'uka* of Kapiolani Boulevard—those would be too trendy, the type of places office workers might go. The bars in Kaka'ako were either some type of strip club, or in some way vehicle related. He cruised past a biker bar—about twenty Harleys parked at a forty-five degree angle along the narrow street. He went farther and slowly passed Club D'Luxe, Heavenly Lotus Blossom, Pussycat Pussycat, and The elDorado.

"How will you know which one?"

"I've got the license number for his pickup. It's a modified Toyota Tacoma."

They turned onto the next block over from Queen Street. Two bars, The Wet Slit and The Rod, shared a parking lot. He saw a grey primer-colored Toyota pickup. It had huge tires, six inches wider than the wheel well extenders, with deep all-terrain tread. Several sets of shocks crisscrossed above the axle and differential and pushed the truck body up—it seemed strangely small in comparison to the tires. The plates read 'BIG TOY.' "This is it," Kai said.

"Jeez. Talk about over compensating. This guy must not have any penis at all."

Kai pulled up in front of the truck, blocking its exit. He positioned his SUV so it was pointed towards the street, or combat parked, in the event he needed to get out in a hurry. Floodlights lit the parking lot, a deterrent to theft and vandalism of the patron's cars. He looked to his left—The Wet Slit. To his right—The Rod.

"This is not the best environment to do an interview. It would be better to get him outside, ideally at the police station. But we can't take him there because this isn't an official investigation."

He looked back at The Wet Slit. The two swinging doors were covered with thick black shag carpeting cut to an upside-down delta. When the doors opened to admit a patron, pink light spilled from the crack. This was the place—he'd replayed it in his mind, retold the events to IA detectives, insurance investigators, and the Officer Involved Shooting Board. He and his partner had sat out here in this same position, but in his partner's SUV. The plan — they'd go in the front door and split up. The person of interest was reportedly inside, but when they pushed through the black furry doors, and stepped past the pink light, it was too dark to make him out.

"This is not a good situation to be in." He looked to the right. He'd never been in The Rod. He didn't know what to expect. Probably dark, loud, and smelling of stale beer. "I should have backup." Even with a partner at The Wet Slit, it didn't stop two people from getting killed, and a third seriously injured.

"Fine. I'll go in," Ka'ena said ready to exit the car.

He grabbed her arm. "You can't go in there—you're under age." If he stepped inside The Wet Slit the bouncer and the bartender would recognize him immediately and play the theme to Hawai'i Five-O, alerting everyone to the presence of a cop. It would have to be The Rod. "Stay in the car. This time I mean it."

He got out of the car and crossed over to the entrance. He pulled open the door and stepped inside.

10

The hot rod theme was seriously overdone. ZZ Top music hammered the air. A drag strip light tree, like one that signals the start of a race, was just inside the door. Beyond that there wasn't much light. Kai scanned the patrons at the bar and the tables—mostly guys in their twenties and thirties, and a few women who were obviously claimed. He felt eyes tracking him as he waked the length of the bar. He stood out. This was a t-shirt crowd. His was the only aloha shirt in the place.

Kai felt confident he'd be able to spot Zack based on the fifteen-year-old pictures from the yearbook. His mother said he was still skinny.

At the back of the bar four men stood around a pool table. The one he recognized as Zack had just taken a shot. His ball rimmed out and he grinned. As Zack straightened up, his eyes caught Kai's. The smile faded. He shifted the pool cue from hand to hand. The others at the table turned their attention to Kai.

"Zack Pizzo, my name is Kai, I'm a police officer. I hate to disturb your game, but if you have a moment, I'd like to have a word with you."

"What's this about?" he demanded.

He could answer him in one of several ways. "I'm sure your mother called to tell you I was coming," was one way, but how many of his friends knew this thirty-year old man lived with his mother? Or, "You know what this is about," and they'd both throw down right then and there and pool cues would be swinging and chairs flying.

"This is about an old friend," was all Kai said.

He locked eyes with Zack. He was probably everything Zack hadn't been in high school or later in life—Kai was athletic, dark haired, with clear dark skin. Zack was skinny and a little stooped, probably from his work, with thinning mousey-brown hair, and pale complexion the texture of a golf ball.

"It'll be quieter outside."

Zack shook his head and gestured with his chin to a nearby empty table. They sat across from each other.

"We found remains that may be Lana's."

"I figured. My mom said you were around asking."

"I'm trying to get a picture of what Lana's life was like—particularly shortly before she went missing."

"She went to school. She did drama—"

"I know all the basics. You walked to school with her every day. What did you talk about?"

"I don't know. Not much really."

"Not much?"

"We walked to school together every day—until that last summer. Then, maybe never. If I didn't work on the sets, I wouldn't have seen her at all."

"Did something happen between you?"

"What is this? Pin-the-tail on the donkey? I cop to something like that and I'm number one prime suspect. Fuck off."

"That's not why I'm asking."

Zack wasn't listening and his eyes had drifted away, looking over Kai's shoulder. They welled up with tears. "I never thought a time would come when I wouldn't see her every day. I thought there'd be forever to say what I needed to say."

The girl was standing next to Kai. She pulled an empty chair from a neighboring table and sat straddling it, with her arms folded across the back.

"Those last few months were unbearable." He was looking directly at Ka'ena. "I would have set myself on fire to get her to notice me. And when she disappeared," he seemed to come up for air before diving back down again. "I thought I'd never see her again."

"I'm not her."

"I know. But I'd forgotten how beautiful she was. I'd forgotten how much—" And when he stopped speaking, ZZ Top's guitars crashed down on chords that were heavy, angry, hurt, and then squealed away like a wounded animal. "She wasn't going to stay, we all knew that. I mean, what would she do? Play the pretty girl in a comedy skit in Waikiki? She had talent. Real talent."

"Could there have been someone else?"

"The school I went to teamed up with Saint Teresa's to do plays. Richard Carvalho, the guy who played Tony, talked about her. He said she was frigid. Kissing her was like kissing a rock. He laughed about it, all the guys laughed. God, I'd have given anything to have kissed her—just once. He said she didn't even want to touch him." He shook his head slowly. "A Maria who won't touch Tony."

"Could something have happened between them?" Kai asked. "Maybe he came on a little aggressive?"

"Could be. We were all horny guys. I didn't really know him. He was a grade ahead of me. We didn't hang out together." He spit the words out. "Carvalho was one of the privileged kids. They had looks, played on all the teams, had money in their pockets, and got all the hot looking girls. Those assholes were set. Probably still are." And the anger in his eyes told Kai that Zack was a million miles from being like them. The closest he got was when he was with Lana.

"Do you know what was going on—?"

"Hey, what are you doing?" Zack directed this over Ka'ena's head. Kai turned to see a big haole guy with a long braided beard hanging two feet down his chin. He was holding a pool cue with two big meaty hands—each finger had a large ring, forming the closest thing to brass knuckles without breaking the law.

"Spoonin' some tush, brah." He was about to insert the tip of the pool cue into Ka'ena's butt crack.

"Get away from me, you fat moron." She swung her elbow and knocked the pool cue away. His buddies were standing to either side.

"Hey, watch it girlie. You wanna' whack a stick? I got a stick for you to whack."

Kai pushed up from his chair, but one of the buddies was directly behind him and punched him in the right kidney. Kai fell forward, catching himself on the table. He reached for his hip, but his weapon was still with the OIS board. He spun and came up, his left hand inscribing a pure arc, his legs straightening, his shoulder rotating quickly. His fist contacted the buddy's chin whose head snapped back, then forward, just in time to receive Kai's right to the upper lip. Buddy's head jerked right then left. Buddy fell back on Braided Beard.

Ka'ena pulled down on the braid and pushed up with the cue—it jammed into the roll of soft flesh behind his chin. Buddy number two was slow to react. He was holding a pitcher of draft, and saving the beer was his priority. But Braided Beard was falling onto him and to keep from being knocked down and losing the entire beer, he sidestepped and lost only half of it.

Braided Beard righted himself and grabbed for Ka'ena. Kai punched him in the gut, which had no affect other than to redirect his attention onto Kai. Braided Beard threw a punch intended for Kai if it could only go through Ka'ena's face. Kai pushed her to the side and she fell towards Buddy Two. A wall of silver flashed towards him. Four ring-covered fingers connected with Kai's left cheek and the pain exploded in his face. He fell backwards, but the table kept him upright. Before Braided Beard could react, Kai hit him with a right to the jaw. No visible affect. Then a left-right-left combination. Braided Beard only seemed to get more annoyed. He cocked back his right hand and the silver glinted as it shot towards Kai.

A pool cue shattered over Braided Beard's head, and the punch lost steam. Ka'ena held the remains of the pool cue in her hands. Braided Beard turned towards her, but Kai picked up a chair and brought it down on top of the bearded one's head. He went down.

Buddy Number Two let go of the beer and reached for Ka'ena. Zack had pushed the table aside and delivered a right into the face of Buddy Two, who took a step back, needing more persuasion to give up the fight. Zack closed in fast. "Get. Her. Out of here," he screamed between punches.

Kai grabbed Ka'ena by the shoulders. She was slick with beer. He half carried her in a bee-line for the exit, going against the flow of people wanting to view or participate in the bar fight.

He got her to the parking lot and unlocked the door of his SUV, pushing her towards the seat. He ran around to the driver's side and got the key in the ignition.

She tried to open the door. "My shoe. I lost a shoe."

"Forget it," he said as he peeled out of the parking lot.

He hung a left at Cooke Street and took it across Ala Moana until they came to the big empty parking lot of Kaka'ako Waterfront Park. He shut off the engine. The adrenaline was still pumping, hearts beating fast. They looked at each other, and slowly they started to laugh. And laugh.

"I thought I told you to stay in the car?"

She shrugged, but they started laughing again. But even while they laughed he knew they could be in deep kim chee.

11

"You smell like beer."

"Aw, that stupid ape-azoid."

He had to get this girl home, but he couldn't take her back smelling like a brewery. What were his options? He could take her to his apartment and she could jump in the shower. Somehow that seemed more dangerous than going back to look for her shoe. There were showers at the park. He used to body surf here, Point Panic, before this was officially made a park. The showers were an improvement.

"There's showers over there, on the other side of that little hill." He pointed to the green mounds that looked like a verdant lunarscape.

She looked into the darkness. "Here?"

"Yeah, just a hundred yards up that path."

She shook her head. "We could get a hotel room."

Okay, so there was something stupider and more dangerous than taking her to his place. "We're not getting a hotel room."

"I know a place. They're okay about it," and she shrugged with a little smile. "They know me."

Why did this not surprise him? "We are not getting a hotel room."

She looked towards the park. "There could be somebody hiding in the bushes. I ain't going in there."

"I'll go with you." He reached for the glove box. She was sitting with her bare feet on the dashboard and his hand went below her legs. He removed a mini-mag light and checked that it worked. He opened the car door and got a towel from his bag. "Come on, let's go."

They walked side by side up the path. He switched on the mini-mag even though the park lights were plenty bright. As they approached the water, the path looped to the right. They cut across the grass—it was darker here. They got to the main pathway parallel to the water's edge and came to a small outdoor shower—three shower nozzles in the center of a low, semi-circular rock wall. She turned on a nozzle and stepped back.

He sat on the wall and laid the mini-mag so it shined on the shower. She took off her t-shirt and tossed it next to him. The white of her bikini top seemed luminous against the dark. "You can turn off the flashlight. It's okay."

He turned off the light. Her back was to him. She pulled down the zipper of her shorts and pushed them down. He turned away. In a moment the shorts landed next to him on the wall, then the bikini top.

The water was splashing. "Brrr, it's cold." More splashing. "Really cold." Even more splashing, then it stopped. Silence. No chattering teeth. No wet footsteps coming to get the towel. No breathing.

"Are you okay?"

No response. He waited.

"Hey, are you okay?"

Nothing.

"Are you still—" He started to turn.

She put her hand lightly on his shoulder. "Relax. I'm right here. I was just looking at the moon. It makes my wet skin look like silk." The towel disappeared from the wall next to him and was soon replaced by a foot. When she'd dried the left leg she took it down and dried the other. "It's the watermelon moon," she said and stepped up on the wall next to him. The towel was wrapped around her. He dared to look up at her, and beyond, at the half moon most of the way to the horizon. It did look like a watermelon sliced in half — the edge was solid white like the rind, but the center was textured with a smattering of seeds. "It's like me. Half of something."

"There's a whole moon up there. You're just not seeing all of it."

She squatted down so their faces were even, her right shoulder grazing his left.

"I lied to you before," he said, not knowing he was going to say this.

She looked deeper into his eyes with the slightest of smiles.

"At Diamond Head. Kila Aki was my dad."

"I knew it. When I saw you surf I said to myself, 'oh, he's one with the wave.' It was beautiful, like a spiritual thing."

They sat in the darkness.

"I lied to you too," she said. "I said I was 'a sexually active fourteen year-old who dreams about violent death.' Well, *most* of it's true." Her hair was wet and an occasional drip coursed down her cheeks to her lips. "Just not the sexually active part." She shrugged. "I guess I've been waiting for someone who can see me, all of me, and not an expectation of me. Somebody that the me that I am is good enough. So while I'm waiting for that person, I'm enduring a slow death by abstinence. I don't know how much longer I can take it. I desperately need saving."

"Come on. Get dressed. I'm taking you home."

"Really?" That tiny little smile. "I was hoping you'd say that." She shimmied into her shorts and turned her back on him before dropping the towel to put on her bikini top. She practically ran up the grass dune as he retrieved the towel and her t-shirt. He tossed her the shirt as they reached the car and she slipped it on. "I knew you'd be the one. I'm so ready. It'll be good. It'll be fantastic, for you too, I promise. I can already feel the fireworks inside. Oh, yes."

What the hell was she talking about? He started the car, turned right on Ala Moana, and crossed Ward.

"Where are we going? You live in Kaimuki."

"How do you know where I live?"

"I went through your glove compartment when you went into the bar."

"What a girl."

"So, where *are* we going?"

"I'm taking you home."

"*My* home? I thought you meant—"

"You thought I meant *my home*?" He shook his head. "Why would you think that?"

"Because we just—" and she went silent.

"What?"

"We just shared an intimate moment."

"Well I hope you don't give it up on the first intimate moment."

Her silence painted the interior of the car black. She turned away from him. They drove along Kalakaua, through the heart of Waikiki and all its lights and crowds of tourists—people who'd paid good money to be packed into one small part of Hawai'i, not even the prettiest part, at least not any more. They passed the low fields of Kapi'olani Park and made their way up Diamond Head along Kāhala Avenue.

He stopped in front of her house. He turned to her. She grabbed her skateboard as she got out and slammed the door. She walked past the Osterlick for City Prosecutor sign and up her driveway. He drove off.

He checked the time. It was almost ten thirty. He headed towards Anna's. Maybe the blond anthropologist was still there, sipping a drink with a little pink straw, glancing towards the entrance. He parked across the street and jaywalked Beretania. The music was loud and the place was hopping. He took the stairs two at a time, paid the cover charge, and got the back of his hand stamped.

He looked around the little cocktail tables for the petite blond with freckles on her nose. He went to the end of the bar. The crowd stood two deep and he checked their faces, patiently waiting for them to turn towards him. He went next to the dance floor—couples bounced up and down to the beat—and near the path to the restrooms and waited.

After twenty minutes he bounded down the stairs and crossed to his car. He drove to McGinty's. The place was lit up and from the street he could hear the raucous laughter and Irish tinged rock music. But he never got out of his car.

He drove home and parked in his assigned spot, facing out.

He climbed the outdoor stairwell to the second floor and walked along the open-air walkway to his apartment. He entered without turning on the light. A blue vaporous aura from the pool deck below reflected on the ceiling. In this half-light he could see the emptiness of the apartment. There was furniture—what was needed, barely: a sofa, a TV on a low shelf, a table with one chair in the kitchen, and a bedroom with a full size mattress on the floor. Next to the door, a surfboard leaned against the wall.

There had been more furniture, but his girlfriend had taken all the good stuff when they broke up. She even took the damn cat. He'd rescued the cat, gotten her her shots, fixed, and patiently explained to the vet's assistant that her name was in fact "Damn Cat." So now there was no damn cat cruising around his legs when he came in the door.

He opened the refrigerator. The light illuminated the kitchen and living room. The shelves were nearly empty but there was one beer on the door. He took it and closed the fridge. He sat at the table and popped open the beer. He lifted the bottle to his mouth but before he could take a sip the phone rang.

12

"Kai?" The voice on the phone was a whisper, but he recognized it immediately.

"Sis?"

"I need your help."

"Where you stay?"

His little sister gave him an address in Kalihi. "Come get me. Hurry."

"If you're in danger, call 9-1-1."

"No can. They come all SWAT, this place gon' blow up."

He didn't like the sound of that. "What's going on?"

"Jus fuckin' come. Go two doors down. The side window. Come strapped." The call ended.

His hand reflexively reached his left side where he normally kept his Smith & Wesson. It was still in the possession of the OIS Review Board, along with his backup. He had nothing.

He jumped into his shoes, ran down to his SUV, and peeled out of the parking lot. He swung onto the H-1 Freeway. He came off at Middle Street and made a quick right onto a small street without sidewalks barely wide enough for two cars to pass. He'd spent three years undercover in this sector and knew the streets and blind alleys well. The houses were often built right up to the road's edge. These were one-story single-wall shacks, of no consistent design. Corrugated sheet metal was often used for roofs and sometimes walls.

He took the next right onto another street of similar size and then a left onto Kamehameha IV Road, a narrow pothole-ridden road that must be taken at five miles an hour. Off of this was Tooms Lane, the street he wanted. It was narrower than most driveways. He drove a car length past it and backed in. At its beginning a large mango tree narrowed the entry. It was late mango season and nearby residents seemed to be without the energy or ambition to pick the fruit. Spoiled, squashed orange mangoes littered the ground. As he drove through it thousands of fruit flies swarmed in the still air.

He turned off his headlights. Gravel crunched under the wheels—loud in the quiet of the night. He stopped the car. He reached under the seat and retrieved his side-handle baton nightstick—a remnant from academy days.

He went on foot. The house ahead had a four-foot chain link fence on the front and side. A brightly colored plastic play area with a slide and a tube to crawl through sat on the patchy front yard. As he approached, a low dark shape moved from the shadows. A dog collar jingled in the darkness. Shit.

He undid his belt, made a loop and coiled it in his right hand. A dog on alert growled low and deep. The fence ran along the side of the house about five feet away. Lights in the front rooms partially illuminated the yard. Loud voices and Jawaiian music from inside hung in the hot, still air. The dog, a brown and white pit bull, was solidly built and had a pissed off look on his face. The growl rumbled louder. The dog's breath stank. Kai walked on the neighboring property, parallel to the fence, moving towards the back yard. The dog kept even with him on the other side of the chain link.

He approached a window, open at the bottom. The room behind it was dark but he could see movement inside.

A whisper from the dark, "Kai? That you?"

"Yeah," he whispered back.

"I'm gonna throw you something. You catch it and get the hell out of here."

"You come too."

"If can. But if no can, you get the fuck down the road. Ready Rough Rider wideout? Don't miss."

A dark shape flew out the window and sailed over the fence. When he caught it he immediately realized it was a baby. The dog jumped for it but was too late and crashed into the fence. It barked and lunged at the fence again, getting his head half way over the top. The child was warm and wore only a diaper. The arms and legs were moving but the child didn't seem upset by being thrown out a window. Kai set the baby on the ground.

He heard voices inside and banging on the interior room's door.

"Jump, Sis."

She was positioning herself to get through the bottom half of the double hung widow. The dog lunged at her and she pulled back. There were voices at the front of the house. The dog jumped at him again and he hit the dog on the side of the head with the nightstick. It lunged again. He stretched open the loop of his belt and put the nightstick through it. Kai jabbed the nightstick at the dog and its teeth clamped down on the end. Kai quickly got the loop over the dog's head and pulled the free end of the belt. The dog squealed at the sudden action then tried to jump back. Kai yanked the belt pulling the dog tight to the fence. It tried to bite his hands but he kept them just far enough away. He wrapped the free end of the belt around the top pipe and tied it to the chain link.

"Come on, Sis. Jump."

She was standing on the ledge and pushed off to get over and beyond the fence. She landed on the ground with a thud and rolled over. She looked large. Why was she wearing so much clothes? He picked up the baby and tried to help his sister up. She looked about eight months pregnant.

Men were running from the house into the front yard. "Hey, motha fucka. Whad you doin?"

They ran for the car. He glanced over his shoulder and saw one man held what appeared against the backlight to be an automatic pistol. "Bring that fuckin bitch back here."

He got the car door open and his sister inside and handed the baby to her. Four men were running towards them, the one in the back had the gun. Kai still had the nightstick in his left hand. He crossed in back of the car and slammed the stick across the bridge of the first man's nose. The man went straight down. The next two backed off. He got into the driver's side and turned the ignition and slipped it into gear. Gravel spit from under the tires. The men chased the car. The one with the gun didn't have a clear shot with his buddies in the way.

Kai gauged the opening to the alley by the trunk of the mango tree. They skidded briefly on wet mango and the car swerved, the rear end just making it past the wall on the opposite side, but the all-wheel-drive kept the SUV under control. He cut left and sped down Kam IV then a right and a quick left.

He made a right at Middle Street without waiting for the light. While he was driving he reached back and pulled the blue magnetic roof light off the back seat, and with his left hand out the window, slapped it on the roof.

"What's wrong with your baby. Why isn't the baby crying?"

"I don't know. Where are you taking me?"

"Queen's Hospital."

"Oh, no. That's gonna jam me up."

"You have to help your baby. Don't you understand that?"

She nodded but moaned from the dread.

"Tell me about the baby. What's its name?"

"Koa. I always liked that name. I want him to be strong."

"Was that the father back there?"

"Oh, no. I ain't seen *him* in a long time. I found someone else to take care of me and the baby."

He got back on the near empty freeway heading east and pushed the car to eighty.

"What were they doing in there?"

"Cookin' up batches of ice all this last week."

"And you stay in the house? The baby too?"

"He won't let me out. I got to take turns on the shake and bake."

"With the baby?" He pulled out his phone and hit the Queen's icon. "This is HPD Detective Ahuna-Aki. I'm transporting to you code two a pregnant woman, twenty-seven years old, and a child, approximately nine months. They've had prolonged exposure to meth lab chemicals."

"Come to the emergency. Stay in your vehicle. What's your ETA?"

"Three minutes."

"Three minutes. Again, stay in your vehicle."

"I knew you'd come," she said softly, "Like when I was at Stevenson and you were across the street at Roosevelt High. That guy that was hittin' on me all the time, and you came over and made him back off. Actually, I kind of liked him."

"You just liked the attention. He was mean to you."

"Yeah, I guess. Still … "

"You fell for guys that bullied you around."

"And you liked getting into fights."

He took the Punchbowl Street exit and made the left into the emergency room driveway. He pulled up next to two persons in white paper isolation suits with full masks.

One opened the passenger door and looked inside. "I'm going to have to take your baby." He reached in and lifted the baby off her lap and put it in the arms of the second white-suited person. The baby was wrapped loosely in white paper and carried through the emergency room doors. Two more white-suited personnel approached the car. One carried booties and instructed Sis to put them on her feet. When she stepped out of the car they wrapped her in a paper robe and put a paper hairnet on her head.

Two white-suited women came to his side of the car and opened the door.

"I was never in the building."

"Just to be on the safe side." the first one said through her mask.

They put the booties on his feet and a hairnet on his head. He stood up and they draped a paper robe around him. He walked between them into the emergency room entrance. They led him to an examination room and one of the women followed him in. "We're going to do a saliva test. Are you okay with that?"

"Let's do it."

The white-suited woman removed a plastic case about the size and shape of a pack of cigarettes. She opened it and removed a swabstick. He opened his mouth and she dabbed his tongue, the roof of his mouth, and his lips. "This tests for methamphetamines, opiates, cocaine, cannabis, and PCP." She returned to the case and took out a second identical swab and repeated the procedure. She sprayed them with a clear solution and watched them turn a pale blue. "Negative and negative. I'm going to do a wipe test on your hands and clothes, to see if you picked up the drug through contact."

She opened another, larger package. It contained a pair of gloves. She removed her gloves and put on this new pair of latex gloves. She opened a small packet, similar to a handi-wipe. He put his hands out and she wiped them, and his forearms. The cloths remained white. "You're clean." She looked through the window to the neighboring exam room. "I can see the young woman and the baby both read positive. You can wait in the lobby, but I suspect they'll be here a while."

It was Friday night and the Queens Emergency Room lobby had filled up. He walked out the automatic sliding doors into the warm night air and pulled out his phone. He called the HPD Drug Enforcement Division to report the house. The shake and bake method was very portable, not requiring the lab set of traditional meth processing, and they may have cleared out already. DE came on the line—a pre-recorded message instructed the caller to call back

Monday morning, or call 9-1-1 if it were an emergency. He called the duty sergeant and identified himself.

"Yeah, well DE works bankers hours. I can ring up the on-call sergeant, but he'll let it wait until Monday. I'll alert the squads, have one creep through the alley. If it looks suspicious, they can sit on the place—that's if we can afford tying up a car. Unless it's obvious, DE's the ones who'll determine if it's a crime scene."

"If it'll help, I've got a witness at Queens ER."

"I'll get a detective over there. You'll be there?"

"In the ER lobby."

"Alright. By the way, Detective Ahuna-Aki. I heard you've been getting some *pilekia* over the shooting. I read the OIS report—something most the guys haven't bothered to do. It was a righteous shoot. The results weren't the best, but these guys who've only pulled their guns out at the range or in front of the bathroom mirror, they don't know what it's like when the shits goin' down. What I'm trying to say is, you did what you did and it was the best you could do. You don't deserve the crap they're slinging at you and I wouldn't blame you if you took the ticket to Washington or Oregon or wherever the hell is recruitin' this month."

"Thanks, sergeant."

Kai went back into the lobby hoping to find someone to tell him how his sister was doing. He recognized the nurse who had drug tested him. She was in green scrubs now and not the white isolation suit and mask.

"Your sister is being showered. She'll be admitted, at least for tonight. A pediatrician will assess the health of the unborn child. The boy is in serious condition. He wasn't responding to outside stimulus—you know, loud noises, tracking movement with his eyes. Also, he looked to be about nine months old, but his mother says he is fourteen months. With that kind of delayed development, we have to call Child Protective Services, for the child's welfare."

"I understand."

He waited in the lobby for over an hour. An HPD detective strode in followed by another man—her parole officer, most likely. The detective waived for Kai to remain seated and went off in search of his sister. The second man followed.

It was another twenty minutes before the detective and the PO returned.

"Detective Ahuna-Aki, I'm Detective Sandoval. This is Parole Officer Reis." They did not shake hands. "You brought her in?"

"She called me. Told me she needed to get out of there."

"What time was this?"

Kai opened the call history on his phone and showed it to Sandoval.

"Had you been there before?"

"No, but I knew the area."

"How long since you seen her last?"

"A few years."

"So you two weren't very close."

Close. As children they slept side by side on the back seat of their mother's car. He'd always taken care of her, gotten her to school safe when other kids picked on her. Then he went to high school and she was still in intermediate. That was the first time he didn't have to watch over her. "After she finished drug treatment I looked in on her for a year or so. She seemed to be doing okay. Then I was on an extended undercover assignment. I didn't see her for a while. We kind of lost touch." She'd become more independent and he'd felt relieved of the responsibility to take care of her.

"Somewhere along the line she got back in the life," the PO said. "She still has another year on parole. This puts her in violation. She'll have to finish out her sentence inside."

"Not to mention the child endangerment charge most likely coming down," the detective said. "That's a couple years added on. She'll lose parental rights over the child, and if it survives, the unborn baby too."

The PO shrugged. "We did what we could. They get caught up in the system, and sometimes the system lets them down."

"Yeah, the system." He knew all about the system, having been in it most of his youth, and now he was a part of it. But the system was made up of people and it was the people who let her down. He'd let her down.

There was nothing left to do. He checked on her condition then drove home.

He kicked off his shoes at the door. With the light off, he crossed the living room and looked out the lanai doors. The pool was too small and oddly shaped to actually swim in and was most attractive at night when no one was using it and the blue light lifted up to the sky.

He took off his clothes and showered, washing off the grit of the day. He dried himself and wrapped a towel around his waist. The bed looked too big. He laid down on the sofa in the dark living room. The pool lights threw shifting, blue light patterns onto the ceiling as if he were underwater. He closed his eyes and in a moment was asleep.

13

SATURDAY

The dog lunged at him, big canine teeth bared. Kai tried to get his hands up but he had no arms. Suddenly a woman appeared between him and the dog. He knew even in the dark that it was Sis. He struggled to protect them both. She turned to him. Ka'ena—her mouth open as if to scream. Instead, a marimba played a familiar burst of notes, then a second time. He sensed the urgency and pulled himself upright and grabbed the phone.

"Kai," he said. The living room was full of morning light.

"You could fuck up a wet dream," Lieutenant Coelho barked at him. "All you had to do was make the notification. 'Some bones turned up. We believe them to be your daughter. The ME will do a positive ID. Sorry for your loss. We'll be in touch.' That's all you had to say and get the hell out of there. Instead you whisked their underage daughter off for a night on the town. She didn't get home till after midnight."

"Ten-thirty."

"That's not the way they tell it. Get over there and pronto. You will apologize to Sara Iwamoto. Do you know who the fuck her husband is? Martin Osterlick, the attorney, for Christ's sake. He's probably going to be our next City Prosecutor. Be there, nine o'clock sharp. I'll meet you in front."

The call ended. He checked the time—he had forty minutes. He brushed his teeth and washed his face. No time for a shave and a shower. He put on a clean pair of jeans and an aloha shirt with colors that said "it's Saturday, my day off."

He got into his car. Something white lay on the passenger side floor. Ka'ena's bikini bottom. Maybe he should return it in front of her parents—maybe not, for both their sakes. He put it in the map compartment.

He didn't want to apologize for keeping her out late. Her mother had given permission for her to be with him. Okay, they went a little past the time. The bigger deal was he'd been asking questions as if he were investigating the murder when the case had not been reopened and assigned to him. But they probably didn't know about that part. So the question would be what was he doing with a fourteen year-old girl until ten-thirty? This is how a suspect must feel when he wants to have a quick chat with his accomplices to get their story straight.

Lieutenant Coelho stood next to a black Mustang parked in front of the Osterlick house. Kai pulled in behind it.

The lieutenant gave him a flat, cold stare and shook his head slowly in disgust. "Come on." They walked side-by-side past the Osterlick for City Prosecutor sign. "The last thing he needs is negative publicity a few days before the primary."

Several cars were in the driveway near the front door. The Mercedes SLS AMG roadster, a sleek, silver, luxury sports car, was undoubtedly Osterlick's. Behind it was a gray Honda Civic that had seen a lot of miles. The third car was a black Lexus sedan with the vanity plates "IMAGE."

When they stepped up onto the entry porch the front door was opened by a young Asian woman who beckoned them in. "You must be the police detectives. Mr. Osterlick is on the lanai, straight through those doors." She looked to be in her mid-twenties, and based on her wardrobe of Chinos and polo shirt with "Osterlick for City Prosecutor" on the back, she was a student or intern working on the campaign. She fit with the Honda.

They kicked off their shoes and proceeded across the living room to the lanai facing the ocean. They stepped onto the travertine pavers and approached the table where Osterlick was finishing breakfast, a cup of coffee in one hand. From this angle Kai could see the transplanted hair follicles on the top of his head. Osterlick was well tanned, booth style, and had eyes with a subtle oriental slant, probably from a face-lift. He was fit from his ersatz triathlon training—treadmill, stationary bike, and heated pool.

Osterlick faced a tall woman dressed all in black, with alligator high-heels, tight pencil skirt, and a well-fitted knit top. Her hair was black, her lips red, and her skin too white for this latitude. She put her hands on her hips. "The offending detective." She looked at him like he was cat puke. "Doesn't he know we have an election in three days? We have no time for bad publicity."

"Well, Coelho?" Osterlick barked. "Is this the man who kept my step-daughter out after midnight? The same detective who was involved in the shooting at the strip club and got his partner killed?"

"Detective Ahuna-Aki is here to apologize," Coelho said to Osterlick. He turned to Kai. "Go ahead. Apologize."

"Ten-thirty. I left her at the gate at ten-thirty."

"I was home last night and I heard her come in after midnight. I know what time she got in. What were you doing with her that late into the night?"

"She wanted to know more about her sister. I took her to see a couple of people who knew Lana."

Osterlick shook his head. "And what right did you think you had to just take her—"

"Her mother gave permission for her to be out until ten. I was a little late getting her back."

"Her mother gave no such permission." Osterlick stood. He was half a foot shorter than Kai. He took up the hands-on-hips power-pose before pointing a finger at Kai. "It's out-of-control officers like him that we've got to weed out. How can we conduct fruitful, efficient investigations when the Department has loose cannons like him?"

"No loose cannons," Coelho stammered. "Detective Ahuna-Aki is taking the recruitment offer from Baldwin PD. It's almost a done deal."

"Good. Let him fuck up in another state. I want him out. Is that understood?"

"Understood," Coelho said.

The woman in black addressed Osterlick. "Luckily there's no mention of it in *The Star-Advertiser*."

"We can handle them," Osterlick mused. "I'm more concerned about *The Weekly*. They feed on rumor. But that rag won't hit the stands until after the election. Will the investigation be reopened?"

"Not likely after fifteen years. Forensic evidence from an autopsy is usually in the soft tissue. All we got are bones. Nothing new to go on."

"Good. We don't need the buzzards circling."

"Will that be all?" Coelho clearly wanted to be out of there.

"You will take care of this." Osterlick said to Coelho. "See that he gets on that plane, even if you have to walk him to the gate and fasten his seat belt."

"Got it," Coelho said and nodded for Kai to follow him out.

"Ten-thirty." Ka'ena strode onto the lanai. She was dressed in jeans with a tattered knee and a black T-shirt with the sleeves torn off. "I got home at ten-thirty. Your car wasn't here. I went for a walk on the beach. I didn't come into the house till after midnight."

"And what were you doing all that time?"

"I needed to think."

"Ha. That would be a first," Osterlick said. "You thought from ten-thirty to midnight? I doubt you could sustain the effort. What do you have to think about?"

"My sister. Who she was, what she was like," Ka'ena said. "And I told him that Mom said to be back by ten."

Osterlick pointed at him. "So you're alibiing this guy? You are grounded. Total house arrest. You do not go anywhere this week. To school and back, no place else. That'll give you time to think."

Ka'ena turned away from him and mouthed "whatever."

"Mr. Osterlick." The campaign worker was in the patio door with a clipboard. "You're first appearance is in Hawai'i Kai at ten. With Saturday traffic we should leave now."

Osterlick stopped in front of Coelho. "I want him gone." He went through the doors to the living room with his consultant and campaign worker right behind him.

"Come on you stupid prick. Let's get the hell out of here." Coelho and Kai walked through the lanai door and across the living room. They slipped on their shoes and stepped out onto the entry porch. The Osterlick team members were just getting into their respective cars and drove past as the two walked up the driveway.

"First thing Monday morning, clean out your desk."

"Are you firing me without cause?"

"I can't do that. The union will be all over my ass. But some friendly advice—get out now, and your life will be a lot easier." Coelho got in his black Mustang and drove away.

Kai unlocked his Outback. A red betel nut skittered across the hood. He looked towards the house. Partly obscured by Areca palms, Ka'ena stood on top the six-foot-high stone wall. He walked closer and looked up at her. "Thanks for taking the heat back there."

She shrugged. "No big deal. I don't listen to him. Besides, I kind of owed you."

Yeah, she did, but he didn't say anything. Seeing her through the palm fronds, she looked right at home, like an animal in the wild.

"My mom wants to talk to you. In person."

14

Why not? It's not like she'd be ruining a good day. He walked through the gate and along the drive. Ka'ena soon joined him, walking barefoot on the grass. She darted ahead and opened the door.

"This way. She has a little room where she does stuff."

He followed her into a room the size of an average bedroom but small for this house. Several worktables were partly covered with fabric samples. A sewing machine was set up on a table against the wall. Shelves held books and framed photographs. Sara Iwamoto sat at a table with a paper pattern in front of her. She was dressed in a gray smock with a paisley scarf covering and containing her hair. She looked like a piece-goods factory worker.

"Thank you for agreeing to see me. I'm afraid I wasn't feeling up to—well, I had too much to drink last night." She shook her head. "I'm trying to cut back."

"Ms. Iwamoto. You don't need to explain anything to me."

"Actually, I do. Martin has his reasons for you to not look into Lana's death—political reasons. You're probably thinking that's self-serving, and you'd be right. I won't apologize for him. When he goes after something—well, just don't get in his way. But I have my own reasons—equally self-serving. I don't think I could go through it again, and it won't change anything."

"But Mom, she was my sister. I just want to know who she was."

"You are different people—*very* different. If she were here today, you wouldn't have anything in common. You probably wouldn't even be friends."

Ka'ena tightened. "Then why do I feel closer to *her* than anyone I've ever met?"

"I'm not surprised. If you would just try to make friends, but you say the vilest things. And the people you do choose to associate with—"

Ka'ena glanced at Kai, then dropped her eyes.

"I shouldn't have said that. It's just that so much has changed," Sara said as if she could look back in time. "Fifteen years ago, the world was bright and full of promise. Since then I've lost two children, first Lana then Chris. I'm different now. I can't see the world the same way—and you've suffered because of it. I haven't been able to give myself unreservedly. A part of me is afraid I will lose you too. But because I've been so self-protective, so scared I'll shatter at the next hit, I've never been able to embrace you, take you into my heart. Every time you push me away I know it's because that's what I've done to you all your life."

Mother and daughter seemed on the edge of tears. He shouldn't be witnessing this. They needed to work things out in private, not with a cop watching. He glanced around the room. On a shelf just above the sewing machine a picture showed Ka'ena and an Army buck private of about eighteen years old. But the Class A uniform had changed around six years ago and this was the old one, so the picture must be of Lana with her brother Chris.

"That was taken about two months before Lana went missing. Our son Chris was leaving for Basic Training the next day. That was the last time he saw her."

"So he was on the mainland when it happened?" Kai asked.

"Yes, Fort Benning, Georgia."

The brother and sister stood shoulder to shoulder, squinting in the mid-day sun. Neither was smiling. In the lower right corner was a date stamp in yellow numbers—September 4.

"Ms. Iwamoto, it looks like there won't be an investigation, at least not any time soon." Kai backed towards the door. "I should be going."

He found his way out of the house. As he walked down the drive he felt her eyes on his back, but he refused to turn around. He was almost out the gate. The pull of her eyes was too strong. He stopped and looked, but didn't see her standing in the doorway, or on the entry porch, or the lawn. He'd been so sure. For a moment he remembered the luminosity of her wet skin in the moonlight. He walked to his car, got in, and pulled away fast.

He hoped he'd never see her again.

15

"Walter D. Shine, Attorney at Law, M – F, 8 – 4 (or by appointment)," was stenciled on the pebbled glass: The doorknob wouldn't turn. He knocked lightly.

Shuffling, muttering, gentle curses from inside approached the door. "Who's there?"

"It's Kai," he said softly.

The door opened. "Kai, my boy. Come in, come in," the skinny, old man greeted him with an enthusiasm that years ago had been genuine but now felt tired. Walter wore his suspenders over a sleeveless t-shirt. His once thick, sun-streaked dark hair was now dry, white, and sparse. A dozen years ago, when he'd been Kai's Guardian ad Litem, he'd had a surfer's lean and muscular torso. Now his chest was hollow and he stood hunched over.

The reception area was full of papers. Stacks of bulging file folders and bankers boxes teetered behind the desk, on top the file cabinet, on every available chair. The desk had only a small area clear enough to do work. The smell of old paper and stale coffee hung in the air.

At one time this room had been the domain of Mrs. Shine. She was every child's image of Santa's cheery wife, Mrs. Clause, complete with gray hair in a bun, chubby cheeks, and rimless glasses halfway down her nose. Anna Shine always found cookies in her desk drawer, and the reception area and Milton's office were kept neat and efficient.

After she died Walter moved his desk into the front room and let go of their apartment. Now he slept in the back and ate takeout food. His white shirts had gotten progressively gray, and he shaved and showered at a nearby gym, but only on the mornings of those increasingly infrequent court dates.

Kai set two cardboard cups of coffee and a box of donuts on the empty spot on the desk. He cleared a chair of its stack of folders. Walter sat behind the desk and took the lid off a coffee cup.

"Uncle Walter, I need your help." Over the next twenty minutes he described the unfolding of events with his sister. "She tested positive, and that's a parole violation. Plus it's likely she'll be charged with child endangerment. I need you to be her lawyer, her advocate, to get her into a program, help her avoid jail time if possible."

Walter looked warily at Kai. "Is there a reason you won't be able to help her?"

"I may not be here. Things aren't looking too good for me right now. If I stay I'll be in a bottomless shit hole with the department. I've been offered a job on the mainland. If I go I can start over, maybe advance."

"This thing with the shooting. You were cleared."

"My partner relied on me, and he's dead now. My sister needs me and I won't be able to help. I need someone to take the point. Someone I can trust."

"I'm honored to be among those you trust—knowing how hard it is for you to trust anyone. What would you like me to do?"

"Review her case, look in on her at Queen's, talk to her PO, and the judge if necessary."

Walter shrugged. "There's not a lot I can do. I can't be her brother."

"I haven't done a very good job of that. She needs someone she can rely on—and it's not me."

Walter rubbed the stubble on his chin. "The truth is, I don't think that's something I could take on." He looked as if searching for the best way to say it. "Right now I'm in transition." He indicated the stacks of paper around him. "That's what this disorder is. I have an intern from Richardson Law School working with me. She's sorting out my files and dividing them up—two law firms are taking over my clients. I'm shutting down the office."

"Wow. I never thought you'd retire."

"I'm not retiring. I'm dying." He shrugged like he'd told a joke that fell flat. "The doctors gave me six months. That was four months ago. At first I didn't tell anybody, didn't do anything to get ready. I saw my oncologist yesterday morning and he said . . ." Walter squeezed his eyes closed. "It could be days. A week tops. More likely days.

"My DNR is on my desk. I've written my obituary, ordered the headstone, made the arrangements. This morning I jotted down instructions for the executor to my estate—such as it is. You're on my list of pallbearers, if you're still around."

This was not possible. Uncle Walter had always been the most solid person he knew—the only adult who'd consistently taken his side all through his youth. "Got ya back, brah," they'd say, but it was really a one sided arrangement. It was always Kai getting in trouble and Uncle Walter protecting his interest, right up until he enlisted in the Marines, and even that was an arrangement to keep a criminal charge off his record.

"There must be something they can do? Clinical trials."

"It's too late for that."

Kai shook his head.

"Organs are shutting down. I have to wear a diaper. My teeth feel loose in my gums. I can only eat soup. I don't have the energy to take on anything requiring a knife. But the worse thing is I smell bad. It's this stink in my nose, a taste in my mouth, all the time, every day. I can't get rid of it. I take a shower and it's still there. I don't know if other people can smell it but—" He shook his head. He looked incredibly tired.

"What can I do?" Kai asked, realizing the answer had to be "nothing," because there wasn't anything he'd been able to do. When his father died there'd been nothing he could do. His mother was killed on the street and he could only watch her die. He'd seen his partner bleeding out inches away from him. He couldn't help his sister, he couldn't hold on to his job, his girl friend, not even the damn cat. How could he help a man die? He'd fuck that up too.

The silence told him Walter thought the same thing—there's nothing you can do, nothing I can do. It's over, the music is fading out.

They sat in the silence. Walter didn't drink his coffee and a donut sat in crumbles on his desk blotter. "It's time for you to get outta here."

Kai nodded and rose. Walter pushed the box of donuts an inch toward him. Kai picked it up and looked deep into his old guardian's eyes. Walter looked away.

Kai closed the door softly behind him.

16

Kai pulled into the parking lot of his apartment building and backed into his slot. He opened the map compartment. The white bikini bottom was on top of his notebook. He climbed the stairs carrying the box of donuts, the St. Teresa's yearbook, the notebook, and the bikini bottom. As he turned at the first landing, he saw someone sitting on the stairs to the next floor—Ka'ena. One knee showed through a hole in her jeans. Her skateboard stood on end between her legs.

"How'd you know where I live?"

"Your registration. When you went in the bar I looked through your glove compartment."

That's right, he remembered. He walked to his apartment door and unlocked it. She followed him in and closed the door behind her. She eyed a six-eight board leaning against the wall and placed her skateboard next to it.

"I thought you were under house arrest?"

"That was my step-father. I told my mom I had to go to the library for a school project. I've just got to be home before he gets home."

Kai set everything on the kitchen table and turned on the electric kettle to make coffee.

She fingered the bikini bottom. "You kept it."

"Take it when you go."

"You can keep em. Put em on your pillow at night."

He took a cup out of the cupboard and set it on the counter.

"I'd like some too."

He took out a second cup and reached for the coffee container. He pried off the lid—empty.

"Do all cops like donuts?"

He opened the refrigerator and looked for a bag of coffee. He went to the little pantry shelves. No coffee.

"I thought it was a joke. The thing about cops and donuts."

"Will you shut up? Just shut the fuck up."

He sat in the one kitchen chair, put his head in his hands, and closed his eyes. He just wanted it to be quiet. He could smell her close to him—the freshness of her soap, her sweat. She was behind him. Her hands gently touched his shoulders and slowly smoothed the muscles. Her fingers caressed the sides of his neck and the tense area behind his ears. How had she learned to do that? Her hands slid down his neck and moved forward across his chest, across his pectorals, brushing his nipples.

He pulled her hands away. "I'm not going to fuck you."

She went around to the other side of the table and knelt in front of him. "This isn't about fucking. You just look miserable and I—I got some pills."

He shook his head.

"For depression. The shrink prescribed them—serotonin."

He faked a laugh.

"I just wanna make you feel better."

He said nothing.

"I can't even do that."

He returned to the darkness of his hands over his eyes.

He could hear her turning the pages of the yearbook, finding the picture from the old neighbor. "She looks just like me," she whispered. "Except she's so beautiful."

Some fourteen year-old boy should roll up on his skateboard and tell *her* how beautiful she is, but then she'd probably pop him in the mouth.

"Somebody killed my sister and buried her in the middle of nowhere, and there's nothing I can do about it. Nothing." Her voice was full of despair. "Do you know how that feels? To be powerless, like there's nothing you can do?"

"Yes." He hadn't meant to say it, but he knew exactly how she felt. He couldn't help his sister. He couldn't help Uncle Walter. He couldn't even help himself. He opened his eyes and looked into hers. "I know how it feels to be powerless."

"You can help me," she said.

He could help her. This was something he knew how to do. And what did he have to lose? He'd be in Baldwin next week. "There's no guarantee."

"I know."

"And you may not like the answer. If you start this you gotta let the chips fall where they may."

"Let the chips fall where they may—as long as it's the truth."

"Sometimes the truth hurts."

"I'm tough. I can take it."

She sure acted tough. But we're not always tough in the way we need to be, and that's why we get hurt—until we build a stronger set of armor, a better line of defenses. "You have to agree to a few things first."

"Like what?"

"We can work on it today and maybe tomorrow. Then we're done. Monday I go back to work. Understood?"

"Understood."

"You'll do what I say. If I tell you to stay in the car, you stay in the car."

"But it worked out last night. I think he said some stuff with me there that he wouldn't have said to you."

"You're under age. You can't go into bars. You could've got hurt."

"You can protect me. Just pull out your gun."

"I don't have a gun."

She looked surprised. "How come?"

"I was involved in a shooting a few weeks ago. They took my weapons while they investigated. They put me on desk duty. It's standard procedure to get one month out of rotation."

"Oh," she said. "So last night, those three meatheads, they coulda killed us."

"Yeah."

"Okay."

"Okay, you'll stay in the car?"

"It was kinda exciting. I dunno. It felt good."

It would have felt better if he hadn't been worried about her. "Be careful. And don't provoke people."

"Me? Provoke?"

He picked up the yearbook and his notebook. "Come on." He headed for the door.

"Where are we going?"

"To the library." He locked up the apartment and they went down to the SUV.

"Can we use the flashing blue lights and the siren?" She was looking at the bubble light on the back seat.

"No. That's for emergencies. We need dispatch approval to go Code 3."

"Code 3. That must be pretty cool flying down the street, jumpin through intersections, making that screeching sound with your tires."

"I guess. I've never actually done it. Only the car out in front goes Code 3. All other cars go Code 2, lights only. If all the cars responded Code 3 they wouldn't be able to hear the other sirens and could crash into each other at an intersection."

He circled the block once looking for parking, but ended up turning in on Likelike Street, a narrow service alley between the Library and the State Archive. He parked along the wrought iron fence and put the bubble light on the dash so he wouldn't get a ticket.

They walked up the front stairs and between the two-story Doric columns, then crossed the foyer and through the courtyard to the newspaper reading room. He asked the librarian for the two local papers for the period Lana went missing. She led them to a microfiche carousel and showed him how to thread the film into the machine and advance the tape.

Kai sat in the chair and turned the dial. Images of newspaper pages flashed on the screen.

"Come on, go faster. You've got a long way to go."

He advanced the tape and stopped to check the publication date.

"This is how you do it." Ka'ena squeezed onto the chair next to him and grabbed the dial. She turned it all the way and the tape spun through the machine, making a loud rhythmic noise. She stopped it with a thunk, checked the date, and sped forward again. She stopped again. It was on the date they were looking for.

On the front page below the fold was the headline, "Kaimuki Girl Missing." They read the story and advanced to the next day's front page. This story was bigger and included a picture of Lana, and quotes from both parents and a few friends. Kai jotted down some notes.

By the end of one week the story had fallen to the back of Section A, and they found no more stories after that. The second newspaper had similar results. They returned the tapes to the librarian's desk.

"Do you have school yearbooks?"

"Yes, for most of the public schools in the Honolulu area."

"And the private schools?"

"Some. What are you looking for?"

"Saint John of the Cross," and he gave her several years.

"I doubt it. That's a small school."

"Would you mind looking?"

The librarian went into a back room.

"Why do you want to look at Saint John's yearbook?"

"I'd like to find more information on the boys she might have interacted with."

The librarian came back with two of the years he had requested. Kai and Ka'ena took the books to a table and sat across from each other. He flipped through the pages and stopped at a picture he'd seen in the Saint Teresa's yearbook—Tony and Maria singing a duet. Tony was played by Richard Carvalho. He was a junior that year so the book didn't give much information on him but he showed up in half-a-dozen more pictures, suggesting he was popular and participated in several school activities.

Zack Pizzo showed up once, in a drama club group photo. He was towards the back, his sunken-cheek, pimple-marked face partly obscured by the shoulder of a taller boy who was standing next to Carvalho. This taller boy would have been Carvalho's friend, and Zack, the scrawny lower-classman behind him, was a hanger-on a few rungs down on the social ladder.

Kai returned the yearbooks. "Do you have Saint Teresa's yearbooks?"

"Oh, no. That one I'm certain of."

Kai thought for a moment. "Do you have Saint John of the Cross going back thirty to forty years?"

"Definitely not. It was spotty for the yearbooks fifteen or so years ago. We have nothing that goes back over twenty years."

He thanked the librarian and went back to the table.

"Why do you want the Saint John's yearbooks?"

"Just an idea. Your mom sent both Lana and you to Saint Teresa's. I'm wondering if she went there herself, and if your father went to Saint John."

"I don't know. She never talked about it. I don't really know much about him. They'd broken up before I was born."

"I'd like to talk to him but you said he's out of state. You don't know him and I can't ask your mom."

"You think my father killed his own daughter?"

It's a possibility, he thought.

Her jaw clenched and her eyes narrowed.

"I want to build a timeline of the events that led up to Lana's disappearance and after. We're limited—we can't interview many of the most important people."

"Didn't the cops who were investigating her disappearance interview those people? Wouldn't it be in a file somewhere?"

"This isn't an official investigation. I can't walk into the police station and get it. But there may be a way to get the next best thing—we could talk to the detectives who did the interviews fifteen years ago."

"Would they remember?"

"Detectives take notes. They have to. Sometimes the trial isn't for months or even years later, so they keep their notebooks."

17

When they were out of the library he dialed Doctor Rajastani's cell phone. "Hi Raj, this is Kai. Just wondering if you looked at those bones—anything you could tell me? Give me a call."

A pushcart vendor was selling coffee under a sheltering monkey pod tree. Kai bought two cups and a pair of chocolate chip cookies. They sat on the broad library steps and popped the lids off the cardboard cups. He connected his phone to the library's WiFi and Googled "Russell Reynolds." Ka'ena scooted close to him to see what he was doing.

"You're Googling my father? Don't you think I haven't done that? There's nothing, except for the newspaper articles we just saw."

He looked over the results. She was right—nothing new. He selected the bookmarked site for the Hawai'i judiciary. If a person had been brought before the courts, either civil or criminal, misdemeanor or felony, they would be listed in this database. Nothing. He set the phone down and took a sip of coffee. "How much do you know about your father?"

"Nothing really. I know what he looks like—looked like. In a drawer in the sewing room, my mom keeps a picture of the two of them. It's the only picture I've ever seen of him. When I was young I used to stare at it, memorizing every little bit of his face, so that if I was on the school bus and looked out the window and saw him I could jump out onto the street . . . " She went silent. "I know, it sounds stupid. You don't get it. Your father was a famous surfer."

"I do get it. I didn't know who my father was until I was fourteen." Why had he told her that? It was something he didn't tell people. He shouldn't tell her any more. She wasn't asking for details, but her eyes, the way she looked at him, he felt she was listening. "My sister, my mom, and I—we lived in a car. Sure, my father was Kilauea Aki." He thought about the legendary surfer with long, white hair flowing in the breeze as he coolly rolled in on a Waikiki wave to the delight of tourists. "But they say he fathered twenty kids. It may be true. He had nine by his wife. A few weeks after his wife died, we went to live with him at his homestead in Papakolea, along with nine half-siblings who didn't much care for me and even less for my sister who wasn't related to them at all. She and I slept in the same room so it wasn't much better than living in the car. My mom changed my name legally to add 'Aki' to hers. A year later he died. Kila had never married my mom so succession of the homestead went to the oldest son—and we were out on the street again."

He left out the next part but he couldn't keep from seeing it in his mind. A week later they were in Ke'ehi Lagoon Park, near where Nimitz Highway crosses the canal. It was night. His mother was conducting business with a man and they'd gone off under the highway. She was always back in an hour—usually less. When she didn't come back he went looking for her. He saw three men running away. He called out, but the traffic from the highway overhead was deafening. He searched the darkness. Propped against one of the highway pylons he found his mother, her dress torn open, her underwear cut away. She was bleeding from several stab wounds. He ran to her and knelt by her side. She took his hand. He wanted to run for help. He wanted to run so far from there and never come back—never see this place again. But she gripped his hand and he couldn't move. She said something but with the noise—he leaned closer. Her breath was on his ear. He struggled to make out what she was saying—these would be her last words to him, he was certain. Take care of your sister? Be a good boy? All he could make out was, "I got you chocolate for your birthday." And she went limp.

The next day he turned fifteen and he and his sister were handed over to Kau Hale o Na Keiki—an agency that takes orphans, runaways, abused, and abandoned children until they can be fostered.

"Did you love him?"

He'd been brought back to the present by this dark-haired, sad-eyed, wild-child sitting next to him and she'd asked a very difficult question.

She pleaded with her eyes. "I mean even though he didn't try to meet up with you when you were young, and you only knew him for a little while—did you love him?"

"Yeah, I did." Kai searched for a reason. "I think he appreciated that I surfed. His legitimate children—the older ones—were fat lards living off his name. The oldest sold surfboards even though he was too obese to surf. The oldest girl was a cosmetologist. She dyed her hair white and used the family resemblance to boost her business. But even before I knew we were related I liked to surf and it gave us a way to connect. We'd grab our boards and paddle out, and he'd introduce me to the guys in the lineup. 'Dis here my boy Kai.' I was so proud. So yeah, I guess I did love him."

She nodded thoughtfully. "And you forgave him?"

"I never felt there was anything to forgive. I can't explain it."

She nodded. "No, I get it."

The phone vibrated and Raj's sultry face was on the screen. He picked it up. "Kai."

"Here's what I've got so far. The body was wrapped in 10 mil Visqueen—like contractors use. That's why the bones were so white in spite of their age. Her arms were folded over her chest. Guess what was in her hands."

"A rosary?"

"Close. A gold chain with a simple cross."

"Sounds respectful."

"My thoughts exactly."

"Anything that might suggest COD?"

"The backhoe disturbed the burial site, tore through the plastic, and damaged some of the bones. I'll keep looking and let you know if I find something."

"Good. By the way, do you have the top sheet for the original missing persons?"

"Certainly. I looked that up when you gave me the name."

"Can you tell me who the investigating officers were?"

He heard her fingers on a keyboard. "Detectives Coelho and Pereira. Coelho, he's your supervisor now and Pereira was your partner."

"That's right."

"Didn't you see their names in the case file?"

"I don't have the case file."

He counted the beats of silence. Three, four, five. "Why don't you have the case file?"

"I haven't been assigned the case."

"What are you doing?" When she was upset, the Hindi accent sneaked in.

"I'm taking a look at the case. Just a drive by."

"Off the books?" she whispered. He heard her get up and shut the door to her office. "Tell me you are not talking to potential witnesses?"

"Just to establish her identity."

"Look. I'm not in your chain of command. But if you compromise a witness, or worse, get a statement without first Mirandizing the subject, you could jeopardize the case."

"It hasn't gotten that far.

"And I shouldn't have given you that information. Forget I said anything. Wherever you are, go home and don't do anything until Monday morning."

"Just a few more things to look into."

"Are you in self-destruct mode? Blowing up your bridges while you're still on them? Go ahead. But don't take me down. I love my job."

"I know. That's why you work seven days a week."

"Don't make this about me—or about us. You've had three live-in girl friends in the time that I've known you—not even a year. Am I supposed to take a number?"

"I thought you were on my side."

"Because of my testimony at the shooting hearing? The evidence was on your side. I just presented the evidence. It wasn't personal."

"Alright. I won't call you again."

Silence. He'd pushed her into a corner and he regretted it. "That would be best." The line went dead. Her picture faded and the screen went to black.

He faced the girl. "We have to stop."

She looked at him as if he'd slapped her.

"The investigating officers—the detectives who worked it fifteen years ago—the lead detective was Coelho." He saw the name meant nothing to her. "My lieutenant. You met him earlier at your house."

"The sphincter-faced guy sucking up to Osterlick?"

"Yeah. Coelho was the primary. He told me to stay out of this. The junior detective, Chip Pereira—" Kai saw a man in his fifties, a few pounds over what he should have been, but still quick on his feet, telling self-effacing Portagee jokes. Uniforms and detectives would stop what they were doing to listen to his stories and laugh. The best partner to have, Kai had thought. He was certainly the most popular, but also an experienced detective. Old school experienced. Street kine experienced. Sometimes Kai would point out that the academy had taught a different way for a given situation. They would discuss it. "If you stop to figure out the ethical thing to do in the middle of a shoot out—you'll be dead," he could hear Chip say. "And if you're dead, then you're partner is dead—or more likely to become dead."

"Pereira." The girl was standing in front of him. "What about Pereira?"

"He can't help us either." His partner's eyes looked back at him from the dark nightclub, his face against the floor, the pool of black blood spreading around him in the dimness. "He's dead."

Her mouth dropped open. He could see her brain processing, coming up with next steps—except there were none. "His notebook. You carry a notebook—maybe he did too. His house, did he have a wife? Maybe she knows where the notebook is?"

"We can't go there for this. It's too soon. She's in mourning."

"That's probably better. She wouldn't have gotten rid of his stuff yet."

Kai shook his head.

"We can ask. If she can't deal with it, we can look through his stuff."

"No," he said firmly.

"No. You're always saying, 'No. Don't go in there. Don't follow me here.' You always park facing out, like you might have to run away in a hurry. Have you ever gone some place without figuring how to escape before going in? You're so fucking gutless." Her voice got louder. "Do you still have a full set or did you lose your balls somewhere?" People outside the library looked over at them. "Last night when I was wet and naked, standing in the moonlight . . . "

He didn't want to be out in the open with people staring, listening. He got up from the steps and walked towards his car.

"Did you feel anything down there?" she shouted after him. "A little quiver? You got anything down there? Or just a couple of shriveled li hing mui?"

He got in his car and put the key in the ignition.

She leaned against the front hood, her back to him.

He started the engine, but she didn't move. If he put it in reverse, she would just back up with him and his back bumper would be up against the library van behind him.

He got out of his car and stood in front of her. "Get out of the way."

"You watched me last night. I know you snuck a peek."

He said nothing.

"I knew it."

"When you dropped your shorts. Just for a moment I saw your tush. Not even a moment. Just a mili-moment."

"And did you feel anything?" she asked softly. "When I was naked behind you in the shower, and you knew I was naked, and then I stood next to you in just a towel—did you feel anything?"

"I felt . . . " But he wouldn't finish the sentence.

"Why can't you be honest with me? That's all I want, someone to just be honest. Tell me how you felt."

He nodded his head. "I felt—something. But I'm not supposed to."

"Because I'm too young?" she asked. "So what am I doing with these feelings? I'm not too young to have them. Am I supposed to just turn them off like a kitchen sink?"

Yeah, that's exactly what you're supposed to do. Turn them off so tight that when it's time to need them you won't be able to turn them on. That's what he'd done. He couldn't tell her that or figure out what she needed to hear. Or what was appropriate to say. And so they were silent.

"Will you take me there? Show me where you found her?"

"Out to Ewa?"

"Yeah."

"Why should I do anything more for you?"

She shrugged as if to say, 'what else have you got to do?'

What was the harm? They wouldn't be talking to anyone. He'd show her a hole in the ground and that's it.

He nodded for her to get in the car.

18

"This is it."

She stepped out of the car and walked towards the pile of dirt and the hole. She stopped about ten feet away and turned slowly, as if suddenly realizing how desolate the place was. She approached the hole hesitantly, almost solemnly. She looked down and sat on the edge, her feet hanging. She pushed herself off, dropping to the floor of the hole. She landed gracefully like a cat, but instead of standing, she laid down.

"Is this how you found her?"

"Yes. Except the ME said her hands were crossed."

She put her hands together on her stomach and closed her eyes.

"She held a gold chain and cross in her hands."

"I don't have a gold chain." She remained motionless for a minute, two minutes. Her eyes popped open. "My mother does," she said. "In a little box. She never wears it."

Tiny rivulets of dirt streamed towards the hole. Small avalanches occurred at the rim.

"Come on. Get out of there."

"I thought I'd feel something. She was here fifteen years. I've only been here a few minutes. Just a little longer."

He found shade by the backhoe and sat. What did she expect to feel? You don't feel the dead. They're gone. At best you'll have some memories—good ones and bad. But in her case, she never knew her sister. The only memories she'd have would be what other people told her.

Fifteen years ago this would have been even more desolate. The closest homes would have been a mile or two away. The ground wouldn't have been stripped of vegetation waiting for development. Tall grasses or wild sugarcane would have dominated the landscape. Wild cane, even without irrigation, could grow taller than a backhoe. A truck with a rig could bring a backhoe from anywhere on the island. Unpaved cane roads from plantation days emanated out spoke-like from the sugar mill. Someone could drive a backhoe a mile or more along a cane road, then turn into the wild cane and dig a six-foot deep hole without anyone around to see.

Ka'ena's hands reached up from the hole. He walked to the edge, gripped her wrists, and pulled her up. She fell against him, then turned away. Her face was dusted pink and tears had made red tracks on her cheeks. The back of her shirt and jeans were red with dirt. She swatted at her legs to get the dust off and a pink cloud surrounded her.

"Let me help you." He went to brush off her back but she stepped away. She leaned against the backhoe and shivered.

"This is it. This is as far as we can go," she said without turning to him.

He knew the answer he should give was yes, but somehow he didn't want to be the one closing the door on her hopes. Why did it matter? He'd made no promises. But there was one more thing. It was probably a waste of time. "Angela Cooper."

Ka'ena looked his way.

"She was a best friend. She lives out in Kapolei. I got her number."

Ka'ena faced him, her eyes bright.

He went to the car and looked through his notebook. Edra Monis had given him the number. He punched it in.

"Is this Angela Cooper?"

"Yes. Well, actually Angela *Culbert* now. Who is this?"

"Detective Ahuna-Aki, Honolulu Police Department. I have a few questions. Can I meet with you this afternoon?"

"And what is this in regards to?"

"Lana Reynolds."

He heard an intake of breath. "Good lord."

"This will only take a few minutes."

"Well, actually I'm not at home. Do you know where the Kapolei District Park is? I'll be on the side across the street from the library. It's my son's soccer game. Look for the blue team."

"I can be there in fifteen minutes."

They got back in the car and drove to the center of Kapolei. The lot at the District Park was full, and street parking was all taken, so he pulled in behind the library and parked illegally at the end of a row. They cut through the library, pausing to use the restrooms to wash the dirt off their face, arms, and hands.

They crossed the street and through the parking lot to the edge of a broad field. Several soccer games were in progress at once, but the one closest to the library was for boys about seven years old. One team wore blue jerseys and black shorts while the other white jerseys over red. Both teams did a lot of running but the ball never seemed to get out of mid-field.

He scanned the crowd of onlookers and focused on a woman in a folding lawn chair with a built in sunshade. She had long blond hair and too red lips. Large sunglasses covered most of her face. She clapped her hands and shouted encouragement to one of the teams.

"Mrs. Culbert?"

"Yes." The woman looked up at Kai and then to Ka'ena at his side. Her red mouth dropped open. To be at eye level with her, Kai knelt on one knee and Ka'ena sat Indian style.

"I'm Detective Ahuna-Aki. This is Ka'ena Reynolds."

"Wow. You should have warned me. I—forgive me, but you look just like—but I'm sure you've been told."

"It's come up."

"And you are Lana's—?"

"Sister. I was born a year after she . . . " Ka'ena looked to Kai.

"I didn't know. I lost touch with the Reynolds. I think they moved."

"Mrs. Culbert, I'd like to ask you a few questions about Lana. You were in a lot of the same productions?"

"Yes. For that year and a half. I was a sophomore when Lana came to St. Teresa's. It was the auditions for Romeo and Juliet. That's when we met. I had a lock on the part. I knew it, everybody knew it, but we had to do readings anyway. I'd already done mine, and I was just sitting back in the orchestra watching the try-outs for the other parts. Then this freshman gets up to read for Juliet. Freshmen never get the leads—it's just not done.

"But then she recited the part. No, recite is not the right word. She spoke those words as if she were living them. I was blown away. We all were. They gave her another passage to read and another. I'm sure they'd made up their minds instantly, and just wanted to hear more for the pure pleasure. It's as if she'd been coached by the bard himself—she drew so much meaning from those words, and did it so effortlessly.

"I thought for sure we'd be bitter rivals, but I was wrong—we were best friends. She was so much fun to be around. It wasn't like she was any more mature than the rest of us, but she knew, absolutely knew, what she wanted to be."

"Did you know Richard Carvalho? He played Tony in West Side Story."

"Yes," and a little smile formed on her lips. "We dated my senior year." She shrugged. "I thought we had something special, but—we went to different colleges and met other people, and you know how things go."

"Do you know what their relationship was like? Richard and Lana."

"Well, they played opposite each other in West Side Story, so all the rehearsals, and when they'd meet in private," she winked. "To go over their lines."

"Was something going on between them?"

"She never said anything. But later I had my suspicions."

"Why is that?"

"I'm not sure. I asked him about it. He came to our 10th Year Reunion. He said the beginning of the summer she was fine, but when school started—ice princess."

"Something could have happened during the summer."

"Her sophomore year she was different. Colder. There was this unfortunate fellow who was totally devoted to her—I don't remember his name. We called him 'Pizza-face.' Pepperoni, I'm sure. Freshman year he and Lana were pals, but after the summer, not so much. She hardly talked to him, like she couldn't bear to look at him."

"Could something have been going on with her and Zach Pizzo? The boy you remember as 'Pizza-face?'"

"*Puhleeze.* Give the girl some credit."

"Could he have forced himself on her?"

"She was two inches taller and in a lot better shape. I mean a lot better. He would have needed to bring two of his friends."

"Did he have two friends? Could that have happened?"

She looked shocked at the possibility. "Maybe, but I wouldn't have known who his friends were." She seemed to consider it. "You know, there was something. I didn't tell the cops before because—well, I didn't really know what I was seeing. But a couple of times, she just up and puked. It wasn't until I got *hapai* with my own and experienced morning sickness first-hand that I understood. I think she was prego. That's why I asked Richard how close they'd gotten."

Ka'ena spoke softly. "And why you wanted to know how I'm related to Lana."

"Yes. You'd be about the right age to be her daughter. I'd always hoped she'd run off to LA to become a star.

When I never heard from her, or about her, I figured she was one of the thousands who end up waiting tables in La La Land. They never make it and are too embarrassed to go home."

"Are you still in touch with Richard? Would you know how to contact him?"

"No. Our circles no longer intersect. I'm married, he's twice divorced, living in New York, looking for the next big score. He's some kind of investment broker. Tried to interest me in derivatives. I said no thanks. He's probably listed with the stock exchange or something."

"Thank you Mrs. Culbert," Kai said.

They stood and walked back to the library parking lot. They opened the doors to the car and the heat poured out. They left the doors open and found shelter from the sun under the meager leaves of a recently planted tree.

Ka'ena looked limp from the heat. "Do you think she was ganged up on by Zack and his friends? That would account for her not talking to him and being pregnant."

"It's a possibility," Kai said. "He told us he never kissed her."

"Maybe he never bothered, the perv."

"He seemed to idolize her. Do you think he lied?"

"Everybody lies sometimes," she said with certainty. "Everybody."

"Everybody? You mean like when you told me you've never met your father and you don't know where he is? That kine lie?"

She looked at him open mouthed.

"If you want the truth, you've got to give me the truth."

She kicked at the dirt. "How'd you know?"

"I suspected, but when you asked me if I loved my father even though he hadn't acknowledged me for fourteen years, that's when I knew—because it's something you're still trying to figure out."

19

"He's not too far from here."

"Where?"

She put her hands on her hips. "If I tell you, will you go get the notes from Pereira's wife?"

"What do you think this is, a game? We're not playing Truth or Dare. This is a homicide investigation. You say you want to know who killed your sister? Then let's talk to the father of the victim."

She stuck her chin out defiantly. "Okay. He lives at the Charity Shelter in Kalaeloa."

Then she seemed to melt. She plopped into the passenger seat. The car was still hotter than the outside. "I should call him to make sure he's there." She pulled her phone out of her back pocket, then dropped it on her lap. It slid between her thighs onto the seat. Her eyes closed and she leaned her head back.

She was snoring lightly. Her forehead was dry. Kai looked at his own arm and saw a glaze of sweat. He reached over, fastened her seatbelt, and closed the door. He turned the air conditioner on high. He drove two blocks to a Fast-Stop and left the motor running while he bought two cold half-liter bottles of Gatorade and a bottle of water, and pulled a handful of napkins from the dispenser.

Back in the car he wiped her brow with a damp napkin. She kept snoring. He moistened the napkins again and wiped her cheeks. Her eyes fluttered open. "I got you something to drink." He handed her a Lemon-Lime Gatorade and she took a few sips, then a few more.

She looked at it as if she'd never seen Gatorade before. She took a few more sips. "I like this. It tastes good." She looked at the bottle as if memorizing the label. She looked at him, her eyes taking a moment to focus, then out the window at their surroundings, then back at the bottle in her hands. "I got sleepy all of a sudden." Her cheeks colored a little.

He knew she didn't want anyone seeing her in a weakened condition. He was the same way. If he fainted in front of his supervisor, he'd jump out a window. "I was really thirsty," he said. "I stopped to get something. Hope you don't mind."

"That's okay." She smiled weakly, deciphering his words. Then as if she understood his intent she looked at him directly and said, "Thank you." She placed her hand gently on his for just a second then turned her attention to outside. Her eyes were tracking now, following a girl walking a frou-frou dog, a man with two twelve-packs of beer pushing open the door, a pickup loaded with five kids in the back. "I should call him to make sure he's there." She reached to her back pocket, found no phone, and was a little surprised to find it on the seat sliding under her butt.

She dialed the phone. "Hi, Dad. I'm nearby . . . Can I come and see you? . . . Be there in five . . . Bye . . . Yeah, me too."

He knew where the shelter was. Twenty years earlier, the Department of Defense had excessed Barbers Point Naval Air Station. The Navy elected to keep a portion for military housing. Some of the buildings were in bad shape and had been built in an era that had permitted aluminum wiring, lead-based paint, and asbestos insulation—the trifecta for expensive rehabilitation or demolition. No developer would touch those buildings and they continued to fall deeper into disrepair. But the McKinney Act gave first dibs for projects to house the homeless and four derelict apartment buildings, formerly Bachelor Officer Quarters, were converted to emergency and transitional shelters for singles and families.

They passed over a small gauge railroad track and through the old gate to the base. As they got closer she grew more animated. "Every time I see him he gives me a present. He bought me new trucks for my skateboard. I told him he doesn't need to do it—he should save his money. He says he wants to. He's got a job—dishwasher at the Disney Hotel in Ko Olina. He can stay at Charity for two years, then after that, there's this program that will help him with rent, as long as he's working—that's good for another two years. By then I'll go off to college somewhere and he said he could find a place near wherever I decide to go. If I want to see him I can just call him up. If I don't, I don't. No pressure. Don't go in the parking lot. Pull around back. You'll see some picnic benches. That's where we meet."

He parked on the side of the road and they got out of the car carrying their bottles of Gatorade. No one was at the picnic tables in the mid-day sun. As they walked to the tables, his phone vibrated in his pocket. He considered not taking it but saw Raj's face on the screen.

"I thought you weren't talking to me." He stepped away from Ka'ena.

"I figured I couldn't stop you," she said. "So the best way to save your skinny ass, and to cover my own, is to help you solve this thing."

"So what've you got?"

"I know how she died."

"What? Are you sure?"

"Pretty sure. There are some ifs built on maybes. But it all comes together."

"Tell me, oh great Rajastani."

"I found two grooves in the left costal cartilage of ribs five and six. The costal cartilage attaches the ribs to the sternum, which is the bone that covers the heart. Something was forced between those two ribs."

"Like a knife?"

"From the profile of the grooves, I believe it was one blade of a pair of scissors. On five it was 4 millimeters and square cut. On the sixth rib it was 6 millimeters and sharp, but to one side. Less than one quarter inch. Several other bones were damaged by the teeth of the backhoe, but the teeth are too large to cause these types of nicks. It had to be something smaller that could *almost* fit between the ribs.

"Here is where the ifs come in. I would need to have the specific scissors, but if they were of sufficient length, they could have punctured the pericardium, a tough multi-layered membrane that forms a sack that protects the heart—something like a gel pack. If it were punctured, or even if it were traumatized by blunt force, it could have resulted in blood seeping into the membrane. This would increase the pressure within the pericardium, thereby increasing pressure on the heart—a condition called pericardial tamponade. As the membrane fills, the heart has a harder and harder time expanding, making each heartbeat less efficient. The person would first feel lightheaded, like they'd had the wind knocked out of them. Perhaps they'd lie down or fall down. The brain would not get enough oxygen and the subject would drift off to sleep. Blood pressure would drop because of the inefficient heartbeat. Without medical intervention, the subject dies."

"What about the blood? Wouldn't there be a lot of blood?"

"Not necessarily. It could be surprisingly little on the outside. The blood is being trapped within the pericardium. That would explain why she still had her school uniform on. If she were bleeding profusely, she'd have pulled off her jumper to attend to the wound. We found a small tear in the fabric over the correct position."

"All that from two little marks on the ribs. Raj, you're fantastic."

"You need to say that to my face," she said, her voice turning husky.

"I will, first chance I get."

"And stop calling me 'Raj.' Everybody calls me that. It's almost an insult, like they can't bother to learn my name. *You* should call me by my given name, Vidya."

"Vidya," he said softly.

The call ended.

He looked up to see a tall, lanky, blond man in his fifties walking from the rear of the building. He smiled and spread his arms wide and Ka'ena ran into them. He gave her a hug and they walked arms around each other's waist to the picnic table where she'd left her bottle of Gatorade. He was holding a pack of cigarettes and a lighter in his left hand, but he made no motion to light up. Ka'ena sat opposite him at the table as if they'd long ago established favorite seats.

Kai approached the man who was still focused on Ka'ena. He could see the resemblance—a similar set to the jaw, a determination in the squint of his eyes. But the man also looked like he'd seen a lot of life. His nose had been broken at some point and not set correctly, and one or more of the many lines on his face was a scar. His hair was long and tied back in a ponytail and he was clean-shaven. He looked up when Kai approached the table.

"Dad, I want you to meet Kai. He's a detective with HPD. He's helping me find out what happened to Lana."

"Good to meet ya." He stuck out his hand. "I'm Russell Reynolds."

Kai set his phone to the record app and placed it on the table. "Mr. Russell Reynolds, I'm Detective Kai Ahuna-Aki, Honolulu Police Department." He showed him his credentials. "Badge number 700914. It is Saturday, September 14," and he gave the year. "The time is two seventeen in the afternoon. The location is the Charity Shelter in Kalaeloa. Also present is the minor child Ka'ena Reynolds.

"Russell Reynolds, you have the right to remain silent—"

20

"Do you understand each of these rights I've explained to you?"

"Yeah."

"Having these rights in mind, do you wish to talk to me now?"

"Why not. I've got nothing to hide."

"Dad, he's a *cop*." Ka'ena turned to Kai. "I can't believe you're doing this."

"I'm going after the truth. Isn't that what you want?"

Reynolds put his hand across the table to hers. "It's okay. I'll talk to the man. How about you give us a little space."

"Fine." She snatched up her Gatorade bottle and stomped away. She came back, hand extended towards Kai. "Give me the keys. For the air conditioning."

"On top the visor." He hoped she wouldn't go for a joyride. She got into the passenger side of the Outback and reached over and turned on the ignition. She leaned the seat back and was out of sight.

Kai put a Miranda Warning card in front of Russell Reynolds and offered him a pen. "Would you please sign at the place indicated and date it."

Reynolds took the pen in his left hand, signed and dated the card, and pushed it across the table to Kai.

In a controlled setting, Kai would ask to search the interviewee, for his own protection, before asking questions. In this case he chose to forgo that step—he didn't want the situation to escalate.

"May I see a picture ID?"

Reynolds reached into his back left pocket and removed a slim wallet. He selected a California driver's license and placed it on the table. Kai wrote down a San Bernadino address and a date of birth. Reynolds was fifty. Lana would have been born when he was twenty, Chris when he was eighteen.

"What high school did you go to?"

"What high school?"

Asking a person their high school was the present-day equivalent of asking for a recitation of genealogy. Do we share ancestors and friends? Who do we know in common? How are we connected? Are you worth connecting with?

"McKinley," Reynolds said, then gave the year. His son was born the same year he graduated.

"And your ex-wife?"

"The same."

High school sweethearts, Kai thought. It couldn't have been easy being pregnant while finishing school. "Did you graduate?"

"I did." After a pause, "Sara didn't."

"Tell me about Lana's broken arm?"

"Her arm?"

Keep Reynolds a little off balance. Ask about easy, but verifiable facts. Broken bones could be checked with the hospital that set them. "Yes, her broken arm."

"When she was fourteen, she broke her arm—the left forearm."

"How did it happen?"

"The kids were roughhousing, Chris and Lana. They grew up playing together. Lana had a tomboy streak in her and Chris got a little out of control—didn't know his own strength."

"Your son, Chris, was two years older. Is that right?"

"That's right."

"So he was sixteen?"

"Yeah, or pretty close."

"What high school?"

"Saint John of the Cross."

"Private school for two kids. Must have been expensive."

"We managed."

"Were you home when it happened?"

"No, it happened after school. I was still at work."

"Construction?"

"Yeah."

"What specifically?"

"Carpentry. Sometimes heavy equipment. I could do a lot of things."

"Backhoe?"

"Yeah."

"And your wife? Was she at home when it happened?"

"No, she wasn't."

Kai waited to see if he would furnish more details. The best way to get someone to talk is to be quiet.

"She designed clothes and had a few women sewing for her in their homes. She spent time with them to match materials, pick colors of thread, types of seams, that kind of thing. Or she'd need to meet with the buyers at the stores that carried her clothes."

"Had she been doing that long?"

"Since high school. She always loved designing, and she was good at it. When we had the baby she couldn't work—I mean go to a job—and still be able to take care of Chris. But making dresses, she could stay home and sew."

"And she made money?"

"Not so much at first, but after Lana, and she got her figure back, she was able to get out to a lot more retailers. She was still young and she'd model the clothes, right there in the store, doing a quick-change in the fitting room. She could've been a model—she had the looks. Sometimes a customer would see her and want to know where on the rack she found that dress." He stopped, as if suddenly realizing he'd been prattling on nervously.

"If you and Mrs. Reynolds were not at home, who told you it happened during roughhousing?"

"Chris admitted it. He was very apologetic. Lana was pretty much in tears—a broken arm is very painful."

"Did you notice a change in their relationship after?"

"Well, you gotta remember she was in a cast for a month or six weeks, so naturally she was restricted in her movements. Chris, for his part, realized he needed to play more gently."

"And after the cast was off?"

"They were still best friends. Hung out together. Did things together."

"Like what?"

"I don't know. The usual stuff. Beach, parties, movies."

"Was Chris good looking like Lana?"

"He pulled my mug. He was okay."

"Popular?"

"Yeah, he got invited to things. Parties."

"Girlfriend?"

Again he shrugged. Was it a tell? A nervous thing he did before answering a sensitive question? "Nobody special. I don't recall."

"How was he at school?"

"Okay. Not spectacular, but he was passing."

"How did his mother feel when he went into the Army—a year short of finishing high school?"

"She was okay with it."

"Someone who didn't finish high school herself, worked hard to put her two kids in private schools, probably wanted them to go to a good college, and then the older one drops out and joins the Army. She was okay with that?"

"Sure she was upset. But he got his GED as a requirement of joining. And he'd get educational benefits."

He's getting defensive, Kai thought. Dial it back, keep him talking about safe stuff. Once he gets to the difficult questions he could shut down. "Did you know Lana's friends?"

"A few."

"Zack Pizzo?"

"Yeah, the skinny, pimple-faced kid. She knew him since intermediate school."

"Edra Moniz?"

"Down the street. They met when we moved into the neighborhood. Best friends since second grade."

"Richard Carvalho?"

A pause. He counted beats, four, five, six. "I don't remember."

"Tony? From West Side Story?"

"Oh, yeah. I didn't really know him."

"Did Chris know him?"

"Probably. Saint John's was a small school."

"Did Chris hang out with him?"

"I duuno. That guy was popular—that's what I remember."

"And Zack Pizzo? Did Chris hang out with Zack?"

The shrug was like the reaction to a small electric shock. "Zack was Lana's friend."

He waited.

"No, he didn't hang out with Zack."

"At Saint John, was there an 'in' crowd?"

"I suppose that's true at all schools."

"Was Zack in it?"

"I doubt it."

"Was Chris?"

The shrug, and then a pause that lasted ten beats. He's thinking, not remembering. "The longer he was there the more popular he became. His junior year he was invited to a lot of parties."

"His junior year. Lana's freshman year."

"Yeah."

"And Lana went to parties with him?"

"Yeah."

"And the beach."

"Yeah."

Easy now, Kai thought. Don't piss him off. He could still be protective of his son, even though Chris is dead. Lana was very attractive and when she was with him, Chris moved up in social status. The popular guys, like Richard Caravalho, wanted *Lana* around, but they were a package deal. He was using his sister. Meanwhile, poor Zack—Lana essentially ignored him during the summer and their second year. The kid who thought he'd have forever to tell her how he felt got left in the dust.

"Parties, beach, movies. It almost sounds like they were dating. Did Chris put a move on her?"

"She was his sister."

"Is that how he broke her arm?"

"You're totally off."

"Come on now. Fourteen and sixteen—that's a little old to be roughhousing. He grabbed her arm and when she tried to pull away it caused a spiral fracture."

"No."

"She told you, didn't she? And you solved the problem by pushing Chris into the Army as soon as he turned seventeen. You didn't want him anywhere near Lana—didn't want him in college and coming home for summer vacation to her. That's what happened."

"No."

"His grades were good enough to get him into college. He'd have submitted applications during his junior year. Am I going to find college applications he put in? His plan all along was to go to college, but something changed his mind. Were you that something? Were you trying to get him away from Lana?"

"You can't prove any of that."

"I can find out his SATs and what schools the scores were sent to."

"Chris had nothing to do with Lana's death. He was in basic training by the time she went missing."

"No, but when you found out she was pregnant, that's when you went ballistic."

"No."

"You didn't mean to kill her. It just happened. And then you used a backhoe to bury her in the old sugarcane land in Ewa."

He was beyond shrugging and could no longer make eye contact with Kai. His fingers were shaking so bad he couldn't fish a cigarette out of the pack. He might be thinking of jumping up and running but Kai was younger. Or fighting—he looked as if he'd had some experience with throwing punches, but again the age factor would be a consideration. Something was going through his mind, that was clear, but what? A story? An alibi? Running scenarios of his past? Of his future?

"Tell me what happened."

Reynolds's jaw was clenched tight. He seemed to be focused on a spot on the table, a chipped piece of paint, a point in time fifteen years past. He was taking too long to answer. It takes time to construct a story when you don't know what the other person knows. Almost certainly the next words out of his mouth would be a lie.

Without looking up, he said in a low, slow, monotone. "I killed Lana."

21

"You're going to have to tell me more. What happened?"

Reynolds looked over at the parked car with his sleeping second daughter. "I was in my wife's sewing room—actually our living room. She cut patterns and materials for her seamstresses. I'd taken apart a pair of scissors to sharpen them. Lana came into the room and said she wanted to talk. She told me she was pregnant."

"With Chris's child?"

"That's what I thought. I was angry, but not at her. I said she'd have to get an abortion. She said no, she wanted to have the child. I said she couldn't risk having a child by her brother—genetic stuff. She said it was another boy's. Now I was really getting angry. I wanted to know who."

"Did she tell you?"

He shook his head. "She said she couldn't—she didn't know which one. There were five or six possibilities. I was stunned. I said something but I don't remember what. It must've been horrible because she slapped me. She'd never done that—never even close. I hit her in the chest. She staggered backwards, but she didn't fall down. I realized I had half a scissors in my hand. She touched the tear in her school uniform and there was blood on her fingertips. She ran to her room. She *ran* like she wasn't hurt at all.

"I went after her. Her door was locked. She said to go away, she wanted to think. I came back in an hour and tapped on the door. She didn't answer. I used a screwdriver to open the door from the outside. She was on the bed. I thought she was asleep, she looked so peaceful—but she was dead.

"I didn't know what to do. Sara wasn't home yet. It was evening. I had a partial roll of plastic from a job site. They use it for moisture barriers under a slab. I cut off a piece and wrapped her in it. I put her in the back of the cab of my pick-up and drove out to the job site—out in Waipahu. The place was closed down but I had access to the backhoe and the truck it came on. I drove to the old sugar fields in Ewa. I dug deep—six feet at least. I figured no house footing would ever get this far down. Maybe only infrastructure, you know, water, sewer.

"I came home. Sara was there. I told her I worked late. She wondered where Lana was but wasn't too concerned—maybe she had rehearsal or set building. In the morning she started calling friends, the school, Queen's Hospital, and then the police.

"We had detectives going through our lives. I guess the family is always suspected. They questioned friends, teachers, neighbors. We put up signs on telephone poles, walked her usual route home, asked people if they'd seen her, looked for something she might have dropped when she was hauled into a non-descript white van. We made appeals to the public, made a video that ran on the news asking if anyone knew anything. Only I knew what had happened."

"You didn't tell your wife?"

He looked up briefly as if surprised by the question then refocused on the spot on the table. He shook his head. "No, no. I couldn't. I couldn't. She was so broken up she could hardly function. You see, the talent that girl had, she was going to have the success my wife missed out on.

"The police had nothing to go on. In less than a week they were shifting manpower, 'reallocating assets,' is what they said. They took men off the case. With no progress the media lost interest and moved on to the next story.

"Our marriage was falling apart. She couldn't or wouldn't communicate, and I couldn't look her in the face. Still, something brought us together, in bed at least. Maybe it was our shattered nerves, or the sense of a bottomless hole inside each of us. By the time she knew she was pregnant with Ka'ena we'd already separated. She didn't tell me until she filed for divorce."

"And you left for the mainland?"

"Not right away. I still wanted to see her, and my new baby. But it wasn't what she wanted. She moved and I had no way of finding her." Kai remembered the difficulty he had locating Sara—it took him an hour or so, but a civilian didn't have access to the DMV database. "I had this fear I would be working a job in Ewa, turning the old sugar fields into tract homes, and I would dig up . . . " He shook his head. "I went to the west coast. Washington first, then a few places in California, wherever I could find work."

"So why did you come back?"

He laughed. "To see Ka'ena. I didn't know where she lived but I knew Sara would send her to a good school. The first day of school I found a place to watch from across the street. Sara dropped her off the first few days and picked her up after school. But that Thursday she came on a skateboard. There was no mistaking her—the resemblance to Sara at that age, and to Lana. I crossed the street to get in her path. She saw me from twenty feet away and her eyes pawed at my face like the fingers of a blind person. She kicked up her board and walked right up to me and put her arms around me. 'I've missed you so much,' she said. It just about broke my heart.

"She wanted to play hooky but I wouldn't let her so we met up after school and got to know each other. She's a great kid, fun to hang out with. Very mature. She definitely has a unique perspective on the world—kind of a raw deal she got, but the world is full of raw deals."

"Did you tell her?"

"No, I couldn't do that."

"But I suspected." Ka'ena stood behind Kai. "Why else would you run away? Then Kai said Lana had been buried and I knew you worked construction—well, I thought you might have done it."

Kai asked, "Why'd you bring me here? You could've just shut up about him."

"We made a deal. You would tell me the truth and I would tell you the truth. And let the chips fall where they may. Besides, I didn't know. He's too gentle."

"I'm going to have to arrest him. You understand that."

"Yes," she said, her eyes boring into his. "And you know I hate you. If I had a gun I'd kill you," she said coldly and deliberately.

"Easy baby," Reynolds said. "I'm gonna go with him. Don't give him a hard time."

"Russell Reynolds, I'm placing you under arrest for the murder of Lana Reynolds." Kai picked up his phone. "End of interview." He stopped the recording.

Kai called the Kapolei police station and asked for transport. He escorted Reynolds to the back of his SUV and had him empty his pockets into evidence bags. Kai handcuffed him and patted him down.

Ten minutes later, a blue and white police cruiser pulled up next to Kai's SUV. The uniformed officer took custody of Reynolds, patted him down again, cuffed him and returned Kai's cuffs, and put him in the backseat of the cruiser. "I'll meet you at the station," Kai said to the officer.

Kai and Ka'ena got into the SUV and followed the blue and white. "I've got to book him. It'll take about half an hour." Across the street from the police station was a Zippy's restaurant. He pulled into the parking lot. "Are you hungry?"

"Yeah, sort of."

He reached into his pocket and pulled out a ten.

"I got money," she said and opened the car door. She reached back in and took his ten and slammed the door.

"I'll meet you here in half an hour," he said through the open window. "Then I'll take you home."

Kai parked in the police parking lot and walked into the station, his badge held in his hand. He caught up with the uniformed officer fingerprinting Reynolds. They did the standard mug shots and another pat down before putting him into a holding cell. Kai transferred the digital recording to a thumb drive and entered it as evidence to be transcribed into a written statement. That wouldn't happen until sometime Monday, but they had three days, or until Tuesday afternoon, to file the charges. He thanked the uniformed officer for his assistance and went to the cell with Reynolds in it.

"Look, you have the right to an attorney. You can evoke that right at any time."

"Yeah, well I'll think about it. You take care of my little girl."

Kai nodded. "I'll get her home alright."

Reynolds grunted.

Kai left the station and walked over to Zippy's. He found Ka'ena with half a burger and fries in front of her. He sat across from her. She pushed the tray towards him.

"I saved you half."

He was going to turn her down but he was starving. He picked up the mahi burger and took a bite. She'd squirted ketchup over most of the fries. He grabbed a few and stuck them in his mouth, licking the ketchup off his fingers. He looked up to see her smiling. "What?"

"Wow. You just eat. No, *oh I've got to wash my hands*. You just go for it."

He looked down at the plate. It was almost empty and he'd sat down only a minute ago. Eating fast was something he'd learned as a kid, when food was hard to come by.

"What I said before," she said slowly. "I didn't mean it."

"You don't want to shoot me?"

"I'll still shoot you, but I won't kill you. Maybe just in the knee."

"I feel safer already."

"I know you had to do what you did."

Did he? He could have just let the whole thing go and her father would be free. No, he had to do it. There are rules, and one of them is we don't kill our children. "I guess."

She reached across the table and put her hand on his.

"It's time to go back."

Kai called the Kapolei police station and asked for transport. He escorted Reynolds to the back of his SUV and had him empty his pockets into evidence bags. Kai handcuffed him and patted him down.

Ten minutes later, a blue and white police cruiser pulled up next to Kai's SUV. The uniformed officer took custody of Reynolds, patted him down again, cuffed him and returned Kai's cuffs, and put him in the backseat of the cruiser. "I'll meet you at the station," Kai said to the officer.

Kai and Ka'ena got into the SUV and followed the blue and white. "I've got to book him. It'll take about half an hour." Across the street from the police station was a Zippy's restaurant. He pulled into the parking lot. "Are you hungry?"

"Yeah, sort of."

He reached into his pocket and pulled out a ten.

"I got money," she said and opened the car door. She reached back in and took his ten and slammed the door.

"I'll meet you here in half an hour," he said through the open window. "Then I'll take you home."

Kai parked in the police parking lot and walked into the station, his badge held in his hand. He caught up with the uniformed officer fingerprinting Reynolds. They did the standard mug shots and another pat down before putting him into a holding cell. Kai transferred the digital recording to a thumb drive and entered it as evidence to be transcribed into a written statement. That wouldn't happen until sometime Monday, but they had three days, or until Tuesday afternoon, to file the charges. He thanked the uniformed officer for his assistance and went to the cell with Reynolds in it.

"Look, you have the right to an attorney. You can evoke that right at any time."

"Yeah, well I'll think about it. You take care of my little girl."

Kai nodded. "I'll get her home alright."

Reynolds grunted.

Kai left the station and walked over to Zippy's. He found Ka'ena with half a burger and fries in front of her. He sat across from her. She pushed the tray towards him.

"I saved you half."

He was going to turn her down but he was starving. He picked up the mahi burger and took a bite. She'd squirted ketchup over most of the fries. He grabbed a few and stuck them in his mouth, licking the ketchup off his fingers. He looked up to see her smiling. "What?"

"Wow. You just eat. No, *oh I've got to wash my hands*. You just go for it."

He looked down at the plate. It was almost empty and he'd sat down only a minute ago. Eating fast was something he'd learned as a kid, when food was hard to come by.

"What I said before," she said slowly. "I didn't mean it."

"You don't want to shoot me?"

"I'll still shoot you, but I won't kill you. Maybe just in the knee."

"I feel safer already."

"I know you had to do what you did."

Did he? He could have just let the whole thing go and her father would be free. No, he had to do it. There are rules, and one of them is we don't kill our children. "I guess."

She reached across the table and put her hand on his.

"It's time to go back."

They walked over to the police station parking lot and got into Kai's SUV. He pulled onto the main road and then onto H-1 to Honolulu. To the right of the highway was the open land that used to be sugar fields, and somewhere an open six-foot ditch where her sister had been buried for fifteen years. She was looking in that direction, as if she could see the spot.

"He lied," she said over the road noise.

"I know," he said. "But he knew a lot of the details. He was involved."

"So if you don't think he did it—" They must have travelled a couple of miles before she finished the sentence. "What are you going to do about it?"

He saw the Aiea exit coming up. He'd taken it half a dozen times with his partner, and he knew the surrounding streets from driving Pereira home when he was too drunk to drive himself. "I want to know what they knew."

22

He pulled up in front of the Pereira residence, a small house tight against its neighbors. A concrete driveway led to a two-car carport that took up half the width of the property. A vehicle occupied every space, with a silver Ford Explorer taking the most favored position near the house. It was the car Chip had driven.

They got out and walked up the driveway to the front door. Before he knocked, a middle-aged woman in shorts and a tank-top came to the screen door. "Kai. What do you want?"

"Hello, Mavis. I hope I'm not disturbing you—"

"Getting my husband killed wasn't disturbing enough? You're going to come by my house now too?"

"Mavis, I'm sorry about what happened. I know I should have come around—"

"No, you were right to not come by here, I might have killed you on the spot. So turn around and get off my property."

"I came to ask a favor. This isn't for me—"

"A favor. You've got some frickin nerve."

"Please, Mrs. Pereira," Ka'ena jumped in. "He's looking into the death of my sister. Your husband worked on the case fifteen years ago when she went missing. He may have kept notes that might be able to help us—help me—find out what happened."

Mavis scowled at the girl. "You should stay away from this reckless prick. He'll help you get a bullet in your gut. That's his specialty."

"Please listen. My sister was fifteen when something happened to her. Fifteen. Your husband talked to people back then—people we can't talk to now. If he kept notes let us take a look at them."

Mavis looked as if she had something sour in her mouth and was about to spit through the screen at the girl.

"Please. This is my last best chance to find out what happened."

Mavis wrapped her fingers around the door handle—to pull the door tighter or to open it? She pushed the door open. "You, not him." She let Ka'ena in. "You'll have to look for it. I'll show you the boxes he kept that stuff in. You find it, you look at it here—and it stays here."

Ka'ena glanced over her shoulder at Kai.

"And you. Get away from my door. Wait down there," and she jerked her chin towards the street.

Kai nodded and looked past Mavis to Ka'ena to make sure she was okay with this. The girl gave a little nod. Kai walked down the driveway and leaned against the passenger door of his SUV.

To find the right notebook would require poring through boxes that most likely weren't well organized. It could be a long wait. There may not even be a notebook. Back then, Chip was the junior detective, the trainee, and would never have been called to testify in court and wouldn't need to refer to his raw notes. But recently, as the senior detective, Chip had required Kai to keep notes and would review them from time to time to see what Kai had thought important. He may have picked up that procedure from Coelho, the detective who broke him in.

Was it possible something else was going on here that they can't see from fifteen years into the future?

A car pulled in ahead of his, and a second directly behind. Two men stepped out of each vehicle—cops by the way they walked. The men were in casual clothes, Saturday clothes. But one of them had a baton—a nightstick with a built in stun gun. Another held a dog toy, a solid rubber ball attached to a foot long nylon rope. When swung it delivered a powerful punch.

The four men approached, two from each side. Kai stepped away from the SUV, but two of them grabbed his arms and pushed him back. The baton was jabbed into his stomach. He tried to pull free.

"You were told," one of them said. The hard rubber ball crashed down on his shoulder. "You were told to drop this."

The two on his flank let him go. The baton jabbed into his stomach again. This time the cop hit the trigger. Kai's muscles contracted all at once and he shook in convulsions. The trigger was released. His body was in near collapse.

"Do you get it? You drop this." The baton jolted into his stomach and the trigger was held for a second, two seconds, three. His muscles tightened fiercely, the lactic acid building up, burning his entire body. He smelled the electric arc and the singeing of shirt and skin.

"Hey," one of them said, and pointed his thumb over his shoulder.

The man with the baton pulled back, and the four men went to their cars. The car doors slammed and their tires squealed. With difficulty he raised his head to look towards the house.

She was there, Lady Liberty, in jeans and t-shirt, one hand raised aloft, her cell phone in hand, thumb pressed to record it all. His legs went soft and he slid down the side of the car until he was sitting on the ground. His body quivered from muscle exhaustion, his jaw clenched tight.

"Come on, we should go." She was bending over him.

He could barely make out what she was saying. She pulled at his arm, helping him up, but his body wasn't cooperating. He tried to talk but his jaw was still tight. She yanked upwards on his belt and he was on his feet, leaning against the SUV. She reached around him and opened the passenger door and guided his fall into the seat. She moved his legs in and slammed the door shut.

She ran to the driver's side and got behind the wheel and scooted the seat forward. She pulled down the visor and got the key, stuck it in the ignition, and started the engine. The car jerked forward and turned right at the next intersection, then left, then right. He swayed from side to side. Soon they were in a cul-de-sac and she looped around the end so the car was facing out. She stopped and put it in park.

"Where are we," he slurred.

"I don't know."

"What happened?"

"When I went in there she made a phone call."

"To Coelho. You find the notebook?"

"Yeah."

"What'd it say?"

"I didn't have time to read it. I took pictures. I'll send them to your phone along with video of those goons."

He gave her his number and in a moment his phone pinged.

The front of his shirt was charred. She undid the buttons. A two-inch-long clear blister had formed on his stomach. He looked away. Don't get sick. The shakes were uncontrollable. He grit his teeth. He opened the door, leaned over, and his lunch splashed onto the curb.

She found napkins and wiped the jetsam off his lips.

Walter was dying, his sister in prison forever. He looked up at the car roof. "*Aaagh,*" he said without wanting to, and tears washed over his cheeks.

His hands were knotted into tight fists. Slender fingers undid the knots, finding a way to hold his hands and also be held.

"I don't get it. She hates you."

"That's about right."

"They all hate you. You're not unpopular. I'm unpopular. You're hated. You were partners with her husband?"

"There was a shooting. He took a bullet." He paused. "It came from my gun."

23

"Your gun? What happened?"

He didn't know how much he should tell her but getting zapped with a few hundred thousand volts had broken down some of his filters. "We were tracking a suspect—a pretty mean guy named Levi Ripozo. We were in Kaka'ako. Levi liked to hang out there. We got a call. Disturbance at the Wet Slit."

"Across from where we were last night?"

"Yeah. The dispatcher said a knife fight. Levi was a knife guy and a bit unstable so we thought it might be him. When we pulled into the parking lot people were running out the door. I asked Chip if we should wait for backup. He said no time. Let's go on in.

"We pushed our way in against the crowd, and went through those fuzzy doors into intense pink light, and then darkness. The music was still blasting. We split up. Chip went along the bar. I circled around to the left behind the tables. The music suddenly stopped and the theme to Hawaii Five-O came on. Now he knew we were there. Someone yelled, 'Levi, there's two of em.'

"He called out. 'Stay back, you fuckin cops.' I couldn't see him in the dark. A few people were still milling around, hoping to see some gore. I pushed my way through. Up on stage, I could just make out a woman, a dancer. The light reflected off the glitter of her g-string and the blade of his knife at her throat.

"The house lights came on. Chip must have got to the bartender. Levi yelled, 'Shut them lights down.' The lights went back off, but in those few seconds, I saw she looked scared. His left hand cranked her left arm behind her back. His right hand pressed a knife to her neck. The door swung open and from the light from the parking lot I could see his position. And he could see us. He could see me leading with my Smith and Wesson.

"The music had been shut down and I heard sirens out side. The doors flew open for a moment and he was looking right into my eyes. We were close—maybe fifteen feet. Then the room went black. 'Throw me your piece,' he yelled. Chip yelled, 'Kai, don't do it.'

"Levi yelled back, 'Do it Kai, or this girl loses her fuckin head.' I glanced over and could see Chip beside the bar, maybe twenty feet away from him. I didn't have a shot, and I didn't think Chip had either.

" 'Throw me your piece,' Levi ordered. The girl screamed a horrible scream. A jet of blood shot out ten feet from her neck. If she didn't get emergency treatment in two or three minutes, she'd be dead. 'Okay, okay. Here's my gun.' I hit the magazine release, but he heard me sliding the mag out. 'With the magazine inside, one in the tube.' The girl was screaming. I slammed the mag back in. 'Don't do it Kai.'

"I de-cocked the gun, put the safety on and tossed the gun towards where I guessed her feet were, so he'd have to move her out of the way to pick it up. I reached down. I kept a small .380 on my right ankle. The door opened and light spilled in. Levi'd pushed the girl aside and she was falling, her hand clutched her neck. He was picking up the gun. Two shots fired from my right—from Chip. Darkness. A shot from the stage and Chip cried. My .380 was out and leveling off at the muzzle flash. Another shot and the impact sent me back against a table and to the floor. I was wearing a vest, otherwise I'd have been dead, but the impact is like getting hit with a sledgehammer. I was on my back looking up and his dark shape was over me. I fired — the first shot caught him under the chin and went up through his brain. I got him two more times before he hit the ground, but he was already dead.

"I yelled 'Clear,' so the back-up and EMS could get in. The doors were blocked open so I could see the three bodies on the ground. There was a big hole in the top of Levi's head. Chip was on his back, grabbing his stomach.

"The dancer was on the floor. I crawled to her and used my fingers to hold the nicked artery together. She was panicking. Blood covered her breasts, her torso. She fixed her eyes on mine like she knew not to let them close or she might never open them again.

"The EMS swarmed around me and they took over. I fell back, still feeling the pounding in my chest. I looked over to Chip. I thought he'd be on his feet by now. I saw the puddle of blood spreading out from under him. I crawled over to him and pulled open his shirt—no vest. He wasn't wearing his fucking vest. I yelled for an EMS. I screamed. The blood was spreading. I was kneeling in it. He was looking up at me. He had a tough face, a grizzled face, the kind that made guys back down quick. But right then he looked scared, and I was scared, and he saw it.

"The shooting review board found I acted with appropriate force. I went lethal because Levi'd already gone lethal. And I acted appropriately in an attempt to protect a life—the stripper's. She made it to the Emergency Room, thanks to the EMS, and was able to testify at the shooting review board from her hospital bed. Chip had violated HPD policy by not wearing a vest. Had he been wearing his vest he most likely would have survived. The department life insurance wouldn't pay out because he hadn't taken basic precautions. His widow got nothing from the policy.

"It was a unanimous decision by the board, but it wasn't a popular decision among the guys on the squad, or any body that knew Chip, or of him, or anybody who wanted to act like a cop in solidarity with his brother cops. Chip was a well-liked guy. Told a lot of funny stories. Was always at the center of any gathering or cookout.

"Me? I'd just come off an extended undercover operation so they'd never seen me at roll call. I wasn't at barbecues, or award ceremonies, or old-timer's retirement parties, or funerals. They didn't know me. All they knew is, I gave up my gun and Chip was shot with it. So yeah, they hate me. They *all* hate me. And I can't say I blame them."

24

Kai moved his fingers and then his arms to gauge his motor control. "I can drive now." He opened the door and got out, and walked stiffly to the driver's side. She threw her legs over the center console and slid into the passenger seat. He readjusted the seat and got in.

The Saturday afternoon traffic into town slowed down when they reached the Middle Street merge. They'd been quiet on the ride in from Aiea, just as well. The stun baton left his muscles drained, as if he'd run a marathon and been a punching bag for a heavyweight fighter. When he was a rookie in uniform he'd ridden with a partner who felt compelled to keep a pleasant meaningless conversation going. Even riding with Chip, when they weren't talking about the case they were working on, the time was filled with stories and anecdotes. He appreciated the time to think. And to pay attention to the road. This interchange worked fine when traffic was flowing, but when it slowed down to bumper to bumper, which was about half the time, changing lanes was a scary experience.

Ka'ena viewed the screen on her phone. "I'll read you the notes."

"Go ahead."

"It starts with the date. 'MP/R Lana Reynolds,' her address and birthday. What's MP/R?"

"Missing Person/Runaway."

She continued to read the notes, which were sketchy. It was comprised of bullet points and incomplete sentences, or sometimes a single word. He misspelled Saint Teresa and a few other words. Some words had to be guessed at. They'd talked to both parents, the neighbor across the street, the teachers, and friends Edra and Angela. Next to Zachary Pizzo was 'BF?' Possibly meaning 'boyfriend'—always a person of interest in teen disappearances.

"Who's Pam Lo?"

"Pam Lo? That name hadn't come up before. Let me see."

She held the phone in front of the steering wheel and his eyes dropped down to read it. "PAM LO, all caps, and a phone number." The first three digits suggested a city government number.

Just then a car pulled ahead of him trying to get to the right lane to exit onto Kalihi Street. He slammed on his breaks and checked his rear view mirror to make sure he didn't get rear-ended. He breathed out.

"You look wiped," she said. "You wanna go and get some coffee?"

"No, I just want to get you home and go to bed." He thought about the misinterpretation the night before. "What I meant was— "

"I know what you mean. Just take me home."

Traffic was slow until they'd passed the Punahou exit. He concentrated on the driving, but the notation of Pizzo as a possible boyfriend kept resurfacing in his thoughts. "Let's run by Zack's place. There's something wrong there.

His mother described Lana as loyal to her friends, but in Zack's case they're best friends one year, and after the summer she won't even look at him."

"You think something happened with them? Maybe he came on to her?"

"Maybe."

"Or he got jealous of someone else?"

"No, I think something happened with *her*. She was the one not talking to him."

He drove through the residential streets of Kaimuki and pulled up at the curb in front of Zack Pizzo's house. They walked side by side to the front door. The sounds of a football game came from the living room. Kai knocked and in a moment, Mrs. Pizzo came to the door.

"You again?"

"We'd like to have a word with Zack."

"I don't think that's such a good idea."

"Mrs. Pizzo. Today I made an arrest in connection with the death of Lana Reynolds."

"Who?"

Kai shook his head and held his hands open.

"It's okay, Ma," Zack's voice came from the living room. "This game—the Warriors' defense is useless." He appeared in the doorway behind his mother. "Why don't we go in the kitchen?"

Mrs. Pizzo let them in and they followed Zack to the table.

"Can I get you something?" Zack asked over his shoulder.

"I'll take that Sprite, if you still got one," Ka'ena said.

Zack pulled a can out of the fridge and filled a glass with ice. He set them on the table in front of her. A large dark-blue semi-circle wrung the underside of his left eye.

"Thanks for getting us out of there last night," Kai said.

"It was the least I could do. You want a beer?"

"I'll take water."

Zack got a beer for himself and ice water for Kai. The three sat at the table and Mrs. Pizzo leaned against the doorjamb.

"Did you know Chris at St. John?"

"I knew him from before, from hanging out with Lana. But I'd see him at school. He was a couple of grades ahead of me."

"Popular guy?"

Zack swung his head back and forward. "I wouldn't call him popular exactly."

"Did he hang out with the cool kids, or was he with the nerds?"

Zack laughed. "It wasn't exactly like that. Each class level tended to hang with their own."

"But within each class there was a social hierarchy, wasn't there?" Kai asked.

"Yeah, sure."

"Someone from a lower class but high social standing had a better chance of interacting with a junior of high social standing than another junior of low social status—was that true?"

"Yeah."

"So, in a way, social standing trumped class level."

"Yeah, I guess."

"So where was Chris?"

"Up the Ala Wai. That's what they used to say. They called it 'shit creek' from when they had that sewer spill. They looked at all of us as being from shit creek."

"Who was they?"

"The ones from Mānoa and Tantalus and Kāhala. The ones with money."

"So you and Chris were of the same social status."

"Yeah. We were pond scum to those guys."

"So how come Chris was getting invited to the parties by the cool ones?"

"He wasn't getting invited for himself. He was getting invited if he brought Lana."

"Lana. Where was she in the social constellation?"

"She was a shooting star."

"So, Chris got invited because he brought Lana."

"He said they were a package deal."

"Did you go to these parties?"

"Are you kidding?"

"You didn't go to a single one?"

"No."

"Don't start lying to me, Zack."

"I'm not lying."

"The statute of limitations is over. And you haven't been given a Miranda Warning. You are safe. Everyone at those parties is safe."

"Safe from what?" Mrs. Pizzo asked.

"Prosecution for Sexual Assault in the First Degree."

"What?" Mrs. Pizzo leaned over the table. "What was going on at those parties?"

Kai addressed Zack. "Were you at any of the parties?"

"No."

Mrs. Pizzo swung her hand and hit Zack across the face. The slap was so quick it made Kai jump. Mrs. Pizzo leaned into her son. "Don't lie to him. I remember you getting fixed up to go to a party. You must have tried on every shirt in your closet. You asked me to iron one. You were so excited. I was excited—my boy was going to be in with the top level, upper-class kids. He was going to get out of this piss-hole place. So don't lie to him."

"I wasn't actually invited to the party. I was with Chris when a junior came up and asked him—and to be sure to bring along his little sister. I said, could I come? He laughed, then he said, 'Sure, come. We can light you on fire and roll you down the hill.' I'd be part of the entertainment."

"When was this?"

"Beginning of summer. Right after school ended."

"And you went to the party."

"Yeah. It was up Round Top Drive. Chris and Lana got picked up by someone with a car. I had to walk from Makiki. It must've took an hour to get there. I was all sweaty, but there was no way I was going to miss that party."

"And what happened?"

"I got to the house. It looked out over Mānoa, Waikīkī, Diamond Head, the ocean—and nothing in between. The house was on a hill and the party was on the bottom level—kind of almost a basement, with one side open to that incredible view. They were playing some kind of Euro-techno-crap, and dancing to it. There was one long room on the downhill side, but on the uphill side was a couple of smaller rooms.

"A guy came out of the room—he wasn't wearing a shirt. He had a big fucking grin on his face and I thought man, there must be ecstasy at this party. I went in the room. The room wasn't that small, maybe the size of our living room, but it was real crowded. People were cheering something on. I saw Chris, but he didn't see me. I tried to push my way in closer to see what was going on.

"I saw another guy without a shirt stagger backwards and a third guy pull off his own shirt and take his place. I moved in closer. Angela was there. She had a drink in her hand and was laughing hysterically, her blond hair flying around her head. I tried to ask her what was going on. She just pointed.

"There was a girl on a bed, completely naked, and this guy was just pounding away on her. I mean just fucking her right in front of everybody, and he was like the third one. And there were other guys lining up. The girl was beautiful, with nice round tits, not gigantic, but good size—I'd never seen a naked girl before, except in magazines. I couldn't see her face, she was turned the other way, but she had dark hair—long dark hair covering her face. And when the guy finished she tried to get up, but they pushed her back down again and another guy got between her legs. She turned her head and she looked at me." He stopped wide-eyed, as if suddenly realizing he'd gotten too close to the edge of a dangerous precipice.

"And you knew who it was, didn't you?"

Zack nodded as if he still didn't trust what he saw.

"Tell me who it was."

25

"Lana," he said, shaking his head in disbelief. "She looked straight at me. She couldn't say anything, couldn't even move her lips, but it was as if she was screaming to me, begging me to help her get out of there.

"I couldn't move. I couldn't take a step forward. I couldn't even raise my hand or yell out to stop. But her eyes—she wouldn't stop looking. Another guy took his turn and the crowd was cheering and moving around for a better view. They pushed me back. I could still see her eyes, even after I was pushed out of the room. I wanted to be sick. I wanted to throw up.

"But I didn't. The music was booming, and everyone was bouncing around the way they do to that kind of music, and then I was dancing too.

"I didn't stay long. I walked back down the hill. I walked home and took a shower and got into bed. I didn't sleep. I could only see her eyes. I still see her eyes."

"And that's when she stopped talking to you," Kai said.

"I wasn't one of *them*, I was her friend. I was supposed to stand by her."

Mrs. Pizzo forced Zack's chair around until he was facing her directly. "You let them do that to her? How could you? How could a son of mine let that happen? You're as bad as them." She slapped him hard, and slapped him again. She wound up to slap him again, but Kai caught her wrist. "She sat at this table," and she pointed to Ka'ena, "Right there. She was as close to me as a daughter—I even thought one day she would be."

"I wasn't strong enough, Ma." His face was red from the slap. "I thought if I worked out, got stronger, bigger, I could . . . " His voice trailed off.

"Whose party was it?"

"Richard Carvalho."

"Was he one of the boys?"

"I didn't see him do it. He was watching, him and Angela. They were right up front."

This was the same boy Lana would later play opposite in West Side Story.

"Every single day, I think of that night. I think of what I would do different."

"And so last night you got your chance to be the hero."

"Yeah." He whispered, as if last night had made no difference.

"I have to get out of here," Ka'ena said. "I have to get out of here *now*." She pushed herself away from the table and ran out the front door.

Kai stood and looked down on Zack.

"What's going to happen to me?"

Nothing, Kai thought—at least nothing he could do. "You're a worm. You will go on being a worm for the rest of your life. All the things you could have had, or could have done, will pass you by. One day your little worm existence will come to a close, and you will wonder if you could have been something extraordinary or done something exciting, but it will be too late."

He walked out of the house. Ka'ena was pacing beside the car, her arms flapping like a fledgling. He expected to see tears streaming down her cheeks, but they were dry. Instead he saw desperation in her eyes. He wanted to put his arms around her, tell her to push it out of her mind, to remember the good things about her sister. He knew none of that would work, and he knew putting his arms around her was not appropriate.

Not appropriate. If she were an injured bird he could pick her up. Or a cat in pain he could stroke her. But a fourteen-year-old girl in anguish — it was not appropriate.

He opened the passenger side door and circled around to the driver's side and got in. Eventually she got in and shut the door.

He drove to Kāhala, but this time he turned into the drive and pulled up in front of the door. "Come in with me," she said as she got out of the car.

Kai followed her into the house.

"Mom?" Ka'ena called out as she headed towards the master bedroom. "Mother?"

"I'm in here," her mother replied.

Ka'ena stepped into the bedroom but Kai stayed a few feet back from the door.

"Mother, we have to talk."

"Will this take long? I'm on my way to the fundraiser. I told you about it, didn't I? It's a rubber chicken affair, but it's the last one before the election. I couldn't decide between the gray suit or the mandarin floral sheath. I decided to go with the sheath. I hope it's not too daring, but you know how Martin is always so monochromatic.

It's up to me to add some color—some panache. What do you think?"

"Kai is here. We have to talk about Lana."

"Honey, that's so far in the past. Before you were born. Don't upset yourself with it. You have such terrible dreams as it is." She stepped into the doorway and faced Kai. She was slender and elegant in the fitted gown based on traditional lines but with contemporary, local-inspired, floral print. "Detective Kai. I should have known she'd run off and find you. I hope you haven't been filling my girl's head with ideas of actually catching Lana's killer."

"Mrs. Iwamoto, we arrested Russell Reynolds for the murder of Lana Reynolds."

Despite her make-up, she went pale.

"He told us what happened."

"Russ?"

"He gave us a confession."

Sara looked from Kai to Ka'ena. "And?"

"I know how she died—and why."

"And who. You said Russ confessed."

"There were a few inconsistencies. He attributed more of the blame to himself than necessary."

"Mom, tell me what happened."

"Dear, I'm running late."

"Please."

"We can talk about it later—when it's just family." She walked past Kai to the front door. She stopped and perched on a bench to slip on her shoes and buckle the straps. She stood, six inches added to her height, and drilled her black eyes into his. "Detective, I think it is time for you to leave."

Kai met her stare. He wanted to look back to Ka'ena to see if she was okay being left here, but to break Sara's stare would seem like a weakness—and he couldn't appear weak to her, not now. "We'll finish this later."

He walked to his car and drove out to the street and turned right, went a hundred feet, made a U-turn, and pulled to the side. In a few minutes he saw Sara's silver Lexus pull out of the drive. He followed her far enough to be certain she was headed to Hawai'i Kai and doublebacked and headed to Mānoa.

He pulled to the curb in front of Grandma Osterlick's house.

26

Kai pushed the doorbell and waited. He could hear the little dog scurrying inside the house. After several minutes, the gray haired woman opened the door partway and looked out.

"Mrs. Osterlick, it's Detective Ahuna-Aki. I stopped by yesterday—"

She looked him over, squinting, frowning, as if she didn't remember. The little dog slipped out the door and was barking at his ankles. Kai bent over and offered the back of his hand. The dog cautiously sniffed, then allowed Kai to scratch him behind the ears. The dog remained quiet and retreated behind the old woman.

When Kai straightened up he saw a faint glimmer in the old woman's eyes far behind the permanent scowl and the embedded bitterness.

"Yes, I remember you. What is your name again?"

"Detective Ahuna-Aki."

"And what did you want?"

"You offered to show me the 'ohana unit, where that dirty girl used to live."

"Yes, that's right. You're going to put her in jail."

"If you help."

She had a verifiable smile on her face. "Walk up the driveway, behind the garage." She pointed to the side of the house. "Go that way. You don't need to come into the house. I'll meet you in the back." She closed the door.

Kai walked up the drive to the garage, and followed the steppingstones around the back to a small cottage, no bigger than the garage itself. Mrs. Osterlick came out of the backdoor of the house assisted by a cane. The small dog ran ahead of her to the cottage. Mrs. Osterlick handed Kai the key ring. He unlocked the door and pushed it open.

The cottage was mostly one large room, with a sofa and an old TV making up the living room area. The kitchen was simple and small. He opened a cabinet drawer—there was still silverware in a white plastic tray. In an upper cabinet he found glasses and plates. The place was very clean. "Has anyone rented the cottage after Sara Iwamoto moved out?"

"No, no, no," she said from the doorway. "Martin said I shouldn't. But I needed the money, so he paid me the rent."

"That was generous of him."

"Yes. And he did it on his city salary. This was before he joined the big firm."

"He worked for the city?"

"Yes, of course. He was a prosecutor. An assistant to somebody or another. He had his own apartment close to work, so to pay two rents must have been difficult. I doubt that woman was appreciative of his generosity. She was divorced, you know."

"He paid the rent even when she lived here?"

"Yes, that's what I said. Then he went to work for those other lawyers and did quite well. He married the divorcée and took her and some other man's child to the house in Kāhala."

He looked in the bedroom. The bed was neatly made, dresser draws empty, paper covered hangers spaced evenly in the closet. No personal items had been left.

"Thank you, Mrs. Osterlick." He stepped out of the cottage and locked the door. He looked at the garage. "Do you drive, Mrs. Osterlick?"

"Oh no."

"Is there anything in the garage?"

"Oh, Martin's car. Some boxes."

"He has a car in there?"

"Yes. It is a garage, after all. He's had the car for—well, I can't really say how long. His first job he saved up."

"Can I take a look?"

"It's all Martin's things."

"I won't touch anything."

"I don't see the point," she scolded. Then she pointed to the keys in his hand.

He selected another key on the ring and tried it on the lock to the back door of the garage. The door opened and the hinge squealed dryly. Whereas the cottage had been bright and open, the garage was dark and cramped. Banker's boxes were stacked at the end wall. The nose of an orange Plymouth Barracuda was an inch away from the boxes. He walked sideways between the car and the wall to get to the front of the garage. He could barely see the rear license plate. MLO.

"I think you should come out now," the old lady called in to him.

He went back to the door. "MLO. Are those his initials?"

"Of course. Martin Lucian Osterlick. He doesn't like 'Lucian.' It means 'light.' I think it's a wonderful name."

He locked the door and handed her the keys.

"You didn't find what you were looking for."

He didn't know what he was looking for. A diary with the bookmark to that night? A handwritten note explaining what happened? The scissors? "No, I didn't."

"No, Martin never seems to find what he's looking for either."

"Martin? Does he come here often?"

"Every few weeks. He says hello to me, like a dutiful son, but he's more interested in something in that garage. I have no idea what it might be."

"Could those boxes contain Sara Iwamoto's possessions?"

"I wouldn't know. I can't reach them, and they look far too heavy for me to lift."

"Thank you for your help." He turned to follow the footstones to the driveway.

"Young man," she called after him. "If you want to look in the boxes, come back tomorrow. If you open a box and it contains his possessions, then you must close it up. But if it is hers—then you can use it however you like."

"Thank you, ma'am."

He got in his car and drove, not sure of his destination. He was without a next step. He didn't have a clue where he would be in a week. It was late Saturday afternoon and couples on the street were on their way to begin their evening together.

He pulled out his phone and scrolled his contact list until he saw Rajastani's face. He touched the screen. After several rings it went to voicemail.

"Hi Vidya. I wanted you to know I took someone into custody for the murder of Lana Reynolds. He'll be formally charged Tuesday. Just a couple of questions. Could a left-handed person deliver the blow? And—well, I'll talk to you soon."

He was in Waikīkī now, driving along the Ala Wai canal—shit creek, to Zack's schoolmates.

The phone buzzed and he saw Rajastani's face.

"Hello, Vidya."

"That's brilliant, a fifteen year-old case closed in a day and a half. Absolutely brilliant."

"Only because of your help. The marks on the ribs?"

"Right hand, most naturally, but a left-handed person could make a similar blow if they swung their arm across their body. So either right or left-handed."

"Okay."

"That wasn't what you wanted to hear."

"I've got a confession. It shouldn't matter."

"But it does—to you. You think you've got the wrong person?"

He tried to answer. Maybe he was just too close to it. Maybe when he got the written statement he'll be convinced. Maybe. He drifted away in his mind, looking for a missing piece that he didn't know the shape or size of.

"Your silence speaks volumes. You said a couple of things. What else did you want to ask me?"

"Would you like to go to dinner with me?"

He heard a little intake of breath, then nothing.

"Your silence—"

"I would love to go to dinner with you—just not tonight."

"Someone else beat me to the punch?"

"No, no, Kai. It's nothing like that. I'm going to a fundraiser—for Martin Osterlick. He's going to be our next City Prosecutor."

"So you want to start the brown-nosing early."

"Brown nosing? I am not familiar with this term." The Hindi in her voice mixed with the Oxford English. "Most certainly my nose is brown—I am from India. But so is yours—you are from Hawai'i. Is this what you mean?"

"No, forget I said anything."

"What is brown-nosing? I can Google it if you do not tell me."

"It is when a person kisses someone's ass so far up the crack that their nose gets brown. That's what it means."

"Detective Ahuna-Aki, that is so offensive. If you were here I would slap you on your face. I cannot believe that you would say such a thing."

"I didn't mean to offend you. It's kind of a joke."

"Kind of—you mean partly a joke, but also partly true? Is this what you mean?"

"Vidya, it's just that I don't like the guy."

"And so you disparage me? I must have misgauged you, and thought you something you are not. In India, we speak of *varna*, our position in life. In America they say we are all equal—but it is not true. There are these subtle gradations and I must have confused you with someone of a similar station as my own. I must go. Please do not call me back."

The connection ended.

27

He parked on South Street near Quinn Lane. He climbed the stairs to the second floor and knocked on Walter's door, then turned the doorknob. The lights were on. The stacks of papers hadn't changed from the morning. Kai moved quietly into the room. Walter was sitting at the desk, his eyes closed. Kai looked to see if his chest was rising and falling.

The gray-haired man's eyes flickered open. Slowly a semblance of a smile crept onto his face. "Kai, my boy. Why are you here?"

"I thought we could swap surfing stories."

"Like when you were sixteen and got skegged by a Brazillian *wahine* here for the Quicksilver. You had stripes across your ass for months."

"I was proud of them."

"The best part was when she tried to apologize—in Portagee. You didn't know what she was saying, and you were too tongue tied to say anything intelligible."

"Hey, I was sixteen and she was, like, wow." He laughed. "She put her hand on the bruises. I never had anything hurt so bad and feel so good all at the same time."

"We can retell them," Walter said. "But we can't relive them. Not me, not you."

"I guess you're right."

"Are you back in rotation?"

"Not yet. I'm working a case off the books. This big time lawyer called Osterlick is in it."

"Martin Osterlick? Be careful."

"You know him?"

"He used to be a prosecutor. He was their best. This was during Arakawa's term as City Prosecutor. When Arakawa retired, he hand-picked Tanouye to follow him. I guess he wanted someone with a heart. When Tanouye got the job, Osterlick was out. He got picked up by a law firm, made partner, and rebuilt the firm."

"Is Tanouye who he's running against in the primaries?"

"Yeah, and a third guy nobody's ever heard of. Because there's three candidates, they have to hold a special election to narrow it down to two. But if one of the candidates gets fifty percent plus one of the votes, they win the whole shebang."

"And they won't have to run in the general election in November?"

"That's right. Here's the thing. On O'ahu, less than fifty percent of eligible voters actually vote in the general election. For a runoff election like this, the number could be as low as fifteen percent."

"So this is the big push."

"To get his supporters to cast an absentee ballot—they can mail it in. It's the more affluent constituents that vote by mail, and that's who he's going after. It will only take about seven and a half percent of the eligible voters to decide this election."

"So there's no real primary."

"The real primary was last year, and it was decided by a twelve person jury. Osterlick and Tanouye battled it out in a trial, and Osterlick trounced him."

"He creeps me out. Let's change the subject."

"Fine with me. Tell me what's going on with you. Who's the girl?"

"What girl?"

"The one you're spending all your time with. Tell me about her."

"How do you know there's a girl?"

Walter tapped a finger to his head. "I just know. Now give."

Kai shook his head. "She's crazy. No she's not. The world she lives in is crazy. I'm surprised she's still sane—although she sees a shrink three times a week. Erratic—she goes from peace to nuclear Armageddon in a second. She's a magnet for trouble, but somehow she gets out of it okay. She gets people to do what she wants—and not by being nice. She doesn't smile, not much anyway. But when she does it just takes you by surprise, like a gift. She demands the truth, but she's willing to lie. She's tough, take no prisoners. But I've seen her cry when—" He was going on and on. Walt smiled. Why did Walt want to know about her?

"Do you think she's the one?"

"The one what? No, she's just a girl."

"That's all she'll be until you let her be more. At some point they have to be more than 'just a girl.' I was hoping I'd get to see that part of your life settled, or at least have hope it would be."

Why bother to explain. If Walt wanted to hear that there was someone in his life, he could give him that.

"She's a special girl. I've never met anyone like her, that's for sure."

"That's good. She sounds like someone you could take a lifetime to get to know." Walter closed his eyes, smiled, and leaned back in his chair. "Kai, do me a favor."

"Sure."

"Turn the lights on."

The lights were on. He looked at his old friend. He felt for a pulse. He put his ear to his chest.

He called the coroner.

28

Sunday

Morning sun reflected off the hood of his car and his eyes popped open. The soft shush of the ocean rose up from one hundred feet below the lookout. The thin white foam lines of the breaking waves moved steadily towards the shore. The sky was light blue over an aqua sea.

She was asleep next to him in the passenger seat, blowing out rhythmic little snores. Her hair was pulled loosely back and held by red plastic barrettes shaped like tiny roses. Her cheeks were pink from yesterday's sun, or perhaps a little blush. She wore a hint of eye shadow and a light lip-gloss, which he only noticed because her face was inches from his.

He'd parked here in the middle of the night and watched the moon over the water—the watermelon moon. He had no idea when she'd gotten into the car, but it seemed natural to look over and see her there.

After a few dozen waves had slid in, her eyelids flickered. One fist clutched at a blue scarf on her lap. Her eyes opened and softly focused on his. She smiled, licked her lips, and closed her eyes. A few minutes passed before her eyes opened again in earnest. "Hi," she said.

"Hi."

She stretched like a cat and straightened up in her seat.

"Where'd you come from?"

"I couldn't sleep last night so I was on my way to early mass. I came by here first—and saw you. I just climbed in the window."

He pictured her pulling up her white dress and lifting her legs into the opening and sliding into the seat. "What would you have done if I wasn't here?"

"Come back after mass."

"What church do you go to?"

"St. Anne's on Wai'alae."

"That's the other way."

Her face said, 'So.' "Why are you here?"

"Because." He wasn't sure why.

"Because there's nothing at home," she said. "You only have one chair. It must get—" She touched his face gently. "You need a shave."

He shook his head. "I need coffee."

She shook her head. "You need a breath mint." She looked into a small clutch and removed a roll of Lifesavers. She peeled one off and put it between his lips.

It was minty, sparkling.

"Would you drive me to church?"

He started the engine and turned onto Kāhala Avenue and took the back streets to Wai'alae. He parked across the street from the church. Families and small groups were coming out the front door. The pastor dressed in a white tunic, thanked the parishioners as they left. "You missed the eight o'clock mass."

She shrugged. "That's not why I come." She opened the door and looked across to him. "Come with me?"

They crossed in the middle of the block, her white dress gleaming in the sun. She adjusted the scarf on her head as they climbed the stairs and entered a side door. He followed her to a pew near the back directly across from a confessional. He sat on the wooden bench while she knelt at the pew.

The pastor approached in the aisle. He caught her eye and looked to the confessional. She nodded, and the priest gestured for her to enter. She left the pew and slipped behind a heavy dark curtain. The priest entered a small door and shut it behind him.

Kai was seated just across from the confessional, and could hear the sounds inside—a shuffle as the small screen was slid open.

"Bless me Father, for I have sinned," she whispered. "I was disrespectful to my mother. I've used bad words. I told someone I would kill him."

"Did you mean it?" the priest whispered.

"I was so angry, but I wouldn't have done it."

"Anything else?"

"I've had impure thoughts. Too many to count."

"You're a teenager. This is a difficult time. Be strong."

"I think my mother is going to hell."

There was a long pause. "It is not for us to judge."

"She did something terrible, terrible, but she won't confess."

"Let her know God's forgiveness is available to all. That's all you can do."

"She killed my sister, and she's letting my father take the blame."

"Oh, child. Bearing false witness—"

"It's true. I know it. God knows it. He has to do something."

The priest breathed deeply. He must await in fear whenever he sees her lined up for confession. "Pray for your mother, and I will pray for you."

"For these and all the sins of my past life, I'm truly sorry."

"Light a candle for your mother, that she may see the light. I won't give you penance—more than you already bear—but try not to sin again."

"Thank you, Father."

Ka'ena parted the heavy curtain and stepped out of the confessional. She seemed lighter. She whispered, "If I die in the next few seconds I'll go to heaven." She waved for Kai to follow her. She went to the front of the church and knelt before a statue of the Virgin Mary. In front of the statue was a rack with small votive candles, a few lit but most unlit. She eased a five from her clutch and squeezed it through the slot, then took a long taper from a sand receptacle and lit three candles. "One for my mother, one for my father, and one for my sister."

"Someone should light a candle for you." He took two dollars from his billfold and slipped them into the slot. He lit a candle in the next row.

She lit the candle next to it. "And one for you." She prayed for a few moments, her eyes closed, her hands pressed together with fingers pointed up.

"You come to church just for the confession."

"It feels good," she whispered back. "Knowing I'm loved even though I'm so very bad."

They've told her she was bad and she believed them. At least she found someplace she feels loved.

After a while she opened her eyes and looked to him. "Coffee?"

They walked up Wai'alae a couple of blocks to a café. A dozen people were in line ahead of them. She kept their place in line while he went to the restroom, washed his face and hands, and ran his fingers through his wild hair to bring it some order. The face looking back at him was hiding the chasm he felt inside—the pain of losing his friend and guardian and surfing buddy, and being too late to help his sister. The face had learned not to express that sadness. He practiced smiling. It didn't look real. He squeezed his eyes shut and reopened them, hoping to see a lighter, happier version of himself in the mirror. He was disappointed.

He rejoined her in line and they ordered their coffee and pastries. "Why don't you find us a table and I'll pay for this stuff."

He watched the baristas work on the line of cups marked with their order. As fast as they finished preparing a drink another cup was added at the other end—they'd never catch up. He looked over the people sitting at the tables with laptops open in front of them or sliding their fingers across the screen of their pads. At one table, a man and a woman facing each other were texting on their phones. In the background, two-decades-old music mingled with the clatter and fuss of the coffee preparation.

He carried a tray and looked around for Ka'ena. She'd found a table on the lanai under a hunter green umbrella. He pushed open the door and approached. She was sitting up straight, her back to him, legs crossed, eyes fixed at a point in the distance as if looking into the future — or the past. She looked mature — not old, but fully developed at a point of perfect ripeness, before any trace of cynicism took hold and the inevitable decay into the putrid beauty of her mother.

When she's ready, or old enough, she could have any boy she wanted. They'll find each other and themselves, and together weave a life of happiness. A wave of loss swept over him and he almost put the tray down and walked away.

At that moment she turned to him, not with a smile, but more like she knew what he was feeling, and her eyes guided him safely to the table.

"I was afraid you wouldn't find me," she said. Her eyes glided along the features of his face the way an artist's brush fills in the lines and shades of a portrait. "And I'd be sitting here waiting forever for you to come. The shop would close, and open and close, and seasons would change, and I'd be sitting here in the rain, and the sun, dried leaves accumulating on the table, in my hair. And you'd never come and I'd missed this moment—what's here right now. You and me."

"I'm here now."

"You're the only person I trust. You know that."

He wasn't sure he trusted himself. His life was a train wreck.

Her eyes, brown with tiny flecks of sea glass and opal, settled on his. "Why are you doing this?"

"You asked for my help."

"But it's getting you into trouble."

"I was already in trouble. I'm near the end of my rope, so I might as well hang myself with the little bit I have left."

"No, really. Why?"

"Because somebody took away a life. She was a girl I might've passed on the street—I could've known. Maybe she'd have made me laugh when I felt junk, or I'd have helped with algebra when she was desperate for an A.

"But instead somebody took that life away, and all that it might've been. And I miss her. *We* miss her. The teen girls standing in front of the magazine racks following her love life or the boys with her poster on the wall across from their beds, and all of us watching as she steps up on the stage to receive her Oscar—we miss her. We'd take our dates to see her latest movie, where she became us, but more beautiful, more vulnerable, more resilient. All that was taken away from all of us."

"If you could, if you had special superpowers, would you go back in time and stop her from being killed?"

He almost said of course, but he saw the dilemma. If Lana had not died, Ka'ena would never have been born. She was the replacement child. It was as if she were asking him to choose. "You deserve to live. But you deserve a better life than you have. You deserve to be happy."

"We could both be happy."

"I don't think it's allowed."

"They can't stop us."

"Yes they can. They can stop me."

She lowered her eyes as if considering his answer. "Are you good at algebra for real?"

"Yeah."

"I need help."

29

"I heard your confession."

"I know. I've sat in that pew. You can hear it all."

"How do you know it was your mother?"

"Every day of my life I see her. She lives with him, sleeps with him, goes to parties and laughs at his stupid jokes. She tries to be the perfect wife—but she hates his guts. I mean skin crawling hates him. And herself, too. What did she do? And now my real father is taking the blame. I'm certain she knows why, and it must kill her. After all these years, after what she did to Lana, and then divorcing my father, and him living like a bum while she lived in luxury, she saw he still loves her. She gave him up to be with Osterlick. Yet my dad was willing to give up the rest of his life for her. That's love. How'd you know it was my mother that killed Lana?"

"It was something your father said. According to him, after he stabbed Lana, she ran to her room. As I understand pericardial tamponade, she wouldn't be running. She'd feel like the wind was knocked out of her. But he said she *ran* because that's what your mother told him had happened, but she was lying.

"He also said he'd taken the scissors apart to sharpen them. He could sharpen them fine still joined together. But if someone wanted to do a good job of cleaning them, say if there was a tiny blood splatter, it would make sense to take them apart and clean the screw and screw hole. I believe your mother did it—probably out of rage, and your dad took your Lana's body and buried her in Ewa."

"I have to talk to my mother."

"So do I."

"Can we do it together?"

"We'll have to. We'll only get one shot at it."

They walked back to the car and got in. The traffic on Wai'alae was busy for a Sunday morning and he had to wait for an opening. Traffic, trying to merge left. What was it? He couldn't put his finger on it. He turned off the ignition.

"You told me something yesterday, when we were driving back to town."

"I read you the notes from the other guy's investigation."

"That's right. Let's take a look at them again. There was something that didn't make sense."

She brought the notes up on the phone's screen. He leaned closer to get a better view.

"Pam Lo," Kai said. "Who is Pam Lo?"

"Why does it matter?"

"I don't like loose ends. Besides it's one of the last entries in the investigation. Make it bigger."

She zoomed in.

PAM LO printed sloppily in upper case, followed by a phone number.

"That's a city number." He took out his phone and dialed the number.

"You think someone will be in on a Sunday morning?"

He shrugged. "Maybe they'll have voice mail."

The phone rang once, twice, three times, four. He expected a voice message but the phone kept ringing.

"What else is in there?"

She slowly scrolled through the notes, their heads nearly together. It must have been on the nine or tenth ring when he heard a male voice on the line. "Adler."

"Hello," Kai said. "Can I speak with Pam Lo?"

"Pam Lo? No one here by that name."

"What office is this?"

"City Prosecutors office. Who's this?"

"Detective Ahuna-Aki." Kai gave his badge number. "What are you doing in on a Sunday?"

"We always keep a staffer here on the weekends, sometimes two, particularly if there's a fast-breaking case. They'll assign a PA to it. You know, in case you guys need help getting a search warrant, or need to be reminded what 'probable cause' means. Usually the calls come in on a different line. You got the direct line to my desk."

"How long have you had this number?"

"Going on five years. How depressing is that? Anyone here past five is considered a loser. I told myself a couple years as a prosecuting attorney and on to the private sector—yet here I am on a Sunday morning."

"Prosecuting Attorney," Kai said. "P. A." He paused. "M. L. O."

"Yeah, we all got initials. Mine's 'PAPA'—Prosecuting Attorney Paul Adler. Don't ask me if I've got kids. Everyone at my pay grade is PA something. Above me is the CP—only one of him, that's the City Prosecutor. Below me are the DPs—Deputy Prosecutors—the first year guys."

"Thanks. You've been a big help."

"Any time."

"I may need to call you back on that probable cause thing."

He ended the call and looked at Ka'ena.

"What?"

"Prosecuting Attorney Martin Lucent Osterlick. Fifteen years ago he was assigned the case."

"Could he have gotten the case dropped?"

"No, but maybe he told the investigators to take it slow. No viable leads, no results, and the lieutenant reassigns manpower."

"But how? I mean, he couldn't just go up to a cop and say, 'take it slow on the disappearance of the Reynolds girl?' I mean, could he?"

"He must have had something on them—or at least on Coelho since he was the lead."

"But why?"

"Sara and Martin went to the same high school."

"He did it because they were *friends*?"

"They *weren't* friends. That's what Grandma Osterlick was trying to tell us. Even in high school Sara was the object of Martin's desire."

"He wanted to *fuck* her?"

"More than that."

"To marry her."

"More. He wanted to possess her, to control her, to be the center of her universe."

Ka'ena screwed up her face and shivered.

"Try Google him."

She did and a long list of articles came up.

"Look for something fifteen years ago."

"Here's something." She opened an article about a case Osterlick had just won. "Wow, look at him. He looks like—" She zoomed in on a picture of the prosecutor. It was Osterlick, but pale, balding on top, and with a noticeable potbelly. She zoomed in tight on the face. The strong, dimpled jaw was missing. "The ugi man."

"Let's look at some more," Kai pointed to an article a year later in *The Pacific Business Weekly*. 'Top Prosecutor Joins TCA.' In the second line of the article he learned TCA stood for Turner Carvalho and Associates. "He went to work for Carvalho. Wanna bet it's the father of the kid with the party? And in another year he made partner, all the while undergoing a self-improvement regimen."

"The triathlon training, the hair implants, the spray on tan. He's still ugi."

"And being ugi is not a crime. His involvement could be explained as a series of coincidences. And your mother, we don't have any hard evidence that contradicts your father's statement."

"Nothing?"

"Nothing. But aren't you concerned about what will happen to her? She could end up in prison. Is that what you want?"

"It's what she deserves after what she did to Lana. And what she did to me."

"You'll be without a mother."

"I'm without a mother now. Besides, it doesn't matter. I'm going to the mainland."

Kai started the engine and pulled out onto Wai'alae. He drove past the mall and turned towards Kahala Avenue.

Kai pulled into the driveway. Lieutenant Coelho's black Mustang was parked next to Osterlick's silver

Mercedes. Kai positioned his Outback nose out. They walked across the paved drive to the entry door and glanced at each other—both understood that trouble was waiting for them inside the house.

Ka'ena opened the front door and stepped out of her slippers. He followed her and kicked off his shoes. Voices came from the living room, but when Ka'ena stepped into the room there was a momentary hush.

30

"There she is," Osterlick's voice barked out. "Young lady, you were grounded for the week."

"I went to church."

"And did a Linda Blair on the altar? Where were you yesterday?"

Kai stepped into the room. Sara was seated with a lime-topped drink by her hand. Coelho stood nearby, the unease creasing his face.

Osterlick pointed at Kai, "And you received a direct order from your superior to stay out of this."

"An arrest was made—"

"And no charges will ever be filed."

"He confessed."

"It means nothing as far as I'm concerned."

"You're not the City Prosecutor."

"But I will be soon, and I assure you, that case will never be tried."

"How would that look—if you drop the murder trial of your current wife's ex-husband where the defendant has confessed?"

"The current Prosecutor will not file it, not because the case is without merit, but because it would have the appearance of an election eve stunt to slander me—a pretty pathetic one at that, since it really addresses a man I barely remember who was married to my wife fifteen years ago. But his inflated sense of right and wrong will overrule his instinct for self-preservation."

A man he barely remembers from high school days? They both knew Sara, but she had picked the tall, athletic, and gentle Russell over the short, intelligent, and ruthless Martin. And ever since, he tried to become the athlete with his triathlon training and fake tans. "Weren't you evening things up? I mean, he was the natural jock and you were the nerdy chess club president. He got to take the prettiest girl to the prom, got her *hapai*. And you? What were you doing prom night? You do know how to hold a grudge, don't you?"

"Why hold a grudge? Clearly I'm the winner." Osterlick opened his arms wide to indicate all of his bounty—the house by the ocean and the understated but expensive furnishings, the successful business and the wealth it brings, and foremost Sara. "I was captain of the debate team."

Yet inexplicably, she preferred one of the dirty children who went to work at a dirty job, like construction.

Sara moved in her chair, perhaps made uncomfortable by Osterlick putting her on a level with the artwork on the walls. Her eyes avoided Kai's, and as far as he could tell, Ka'ena's. If he put the pressure on her, in a different way, maybe she would say something.

"Sara, don't you want justice for your daughter?"

"Don't answer him," Osterlick said, then snarled at him. "And you do not address her or any member of this family. Your renegade investigation is over."

"No justice for what was done to her?"

Her eyes snapped to his. Her mouth opened but closed as if obeying a silent command.

"I will get a court order preventing you from harassing any member of my family. You will not contact this girl."

Ka'ena's back stiffened. "Fuck you. I'll talk to whoever I want to."

"Because she is underage, and psychologically fragile—after all, she does see a shrink three times a week. The courts want to protect such susceptible children from those who would prey on them."

"I have a witness who will testify what happened at Carvalho's party."

"Martin?" Sara looked to her husband.

"You have nothing but hearsay. And if you pursue this, you will find yourself looking at several felony charges, including abuse of power, endangering a minor, corrupting the morals of a minor. I'm sure we could indict for sexual assault of a minor. Even if it doesn't stand, imagine the ride you'll get in prison—a kiddy diddler and an ex-cop. Ouch."

"He never touched me, you bastard."

Osterlick laughed. "Given enough time I'm sure I could find a dozen witnesses that put the two of you together in, shall we say, compromising positions."

Kai thought of the bar, carrying her out, the beach park, her showing up at his apartment, the conversation on the library steps. All out in the open, all may have witnesses.

"Besides," Osterlick continued. "This young detective is the bastard. I, on the other hand, am an asshole—a quality much appreciated in a lawyer." He smiled at Kai.

"And I'm about to rain some serious shit down on you. And your family."

He knew about Sis.

"And I could make her life very, very uncomfortable."

And his years of getting in fights to protect her were not over.

"So just shut your mouth, Detective. Stay away from my family, and get on that big jet plane headed for Baldwin, Washington. Leave the surfboard and take up snowboarding. Buy yourself a little house. Your money will go farther there. Get yourself a little honey—one of legal age. Settle into a nice cushy job. Plenty of opportunities for advancement. Most importantly, no past to haunt you."

Kai looked around the room. Osterlick held a little smile. He was having fun. Kai was a cat toy to him, dangling from a string, getting swatted and clawed. Slowly he'll pull the stuffing out, but Kai will still be dangling, lifeless. Sara Iwamoto's eyes reflected the knowledge that the last chance she'd be found to be responsible for her daughter's death was fading away. But if she knew about the party the last possibility of accounting for the rape of her daughter was also slipping away.

Coelho was present through all of this. He didn't flinch at the mention of the Carvalho party. Osterlick had talked openly in front of him. Did he know about it? He must know. Had he known all along? Chip too? They came across it when investigating Lana's disappearance but chose to keep it quiet—why? And why go to Osterlick? To broker a deal with Carvalho? Somehow a deal was struck, progress slowed, and the investigation shut down. What did Osterlick have on him? Whatever it was, it still had a hold on him.

"Listen to him, Kai," Coelho said. "Just go out the door. It didn't work out here. Make a new life someplace else."

His life since the shooting—questions, sidelong looks. No one trusted him, no one believed him.

Ka'ena was staring at him. She trusted him. Somehow, this misguided child believed in him. But then she was susceptible, fragile, vulnerable.

Kai took a step back towards the door.

Her eyes screamed at him to stay. He looked away.

He took another step back.

Coelho took a full breath for the first time since he'd entered the room.

Kai sneaked a glance at the girl he would never see again. She gasped. She'd been stabbed in the heart.

He turned to the door, grabbed his shoes, walked barefoot to his car, and drove off.

31

At the end of the driveway, he looked left towards home—one chair and no damn cat.

He turned right, drove one hundred yards, and made a U. A clump of Areca palms partially obscured his car. He reached into the glove compartment and retrieved the compact binoculars and adjusted them, keeping them ready on the dashboard. He put on his shoes and waited.

He spent the time looking at Chip Pereira's case notes but didn't spot anything new or helpful. After twenty minutes, Coelho's black Mustang drove out of the Osterlick gate and turned left. Kai wasn't going to follow him. He knew he'd see Coelho in the morning at the detective squad.

What could Osterlick have on Coelho? It had to be good to put the lid on a missing person investigation. And it had to be durable—with no statute of limitations, like murder. Or ongoing, something Coelho can't bring himself to stop because he's addicted or because it makes him too much money. He didn't know Coelho that well, but didn't think he had a substance abuse problem. Gambling? Osterlick might be able to help him out financially now, but fifteen years ago when he was a prosecuting attorney—not likely.

After another hour the silver Mercedes went out the gate. Kai used the binoculars to confirm it was Martin Osterlick at the wheel. The Mercedes turned left onto Kahala Avenue and was soon out of sight. Kai started his engine and drove up to the gate and turned in, parking his Outback as he did before, nose pointed out.

He was barely out of his car when he saw the front door open and Ka'ena running towards him barefoot, white dress billowing. She stopped short a few feet in front of him.

"I knew you'd come back. At first I doubted. I couldn't believe it, you walking out, leaving me. But I knew you wouldn't. I knew it."

"I have to talk to your mom."

"I don't think that's possible right now," and gestured like she was drinking from a bottle.

Kai shook his head. Any statement gotten while she was under the influence of alcohol or drugs would be useless.

"I was packing a bag—just one. I can't stay here, knowing she killed my sister, and Osterlick is some kind of fucking monster. I figured I'd get a round trip ticket to Las Vegas, one of those package deals. I've got enough cash. Of course I won't actually stay in Vegas. I'll hitchhike north, to Washington. I'll meet up with you there." She shrugged, not sure he would like this part of her plan, but went ahead. "I'll stay with you. I won't bother you about doing it—not until I turn eighteen, or maybe sixteen. Then we can decide."

"I'm going to finish this."

"It's finished. They won. Game over."

He shook his head. "Not yet. Let me see your mom," he said as he walked to the front door.

She ran ahead of him, leading him to the living room. Sara was in the same chair he'd seen her in earlier, slumped down a little, listing to one side. Her eyes were closed and she was snoring.

"Ms. Iwamoto. Sara."

She opened her eyes and attempted to sit up straight, then gave up on the effort. "Who?"

"Mom, it's Detective Kai."

"Oh, the cute one." She smiled as she looked at him. "I think my daughter," she wagged a finger, "has a crush on you. Don't you, dear?"

"Mom, please."

"Sara. I need to talk to you about something. But it's very important that you just listen. Don't say anything. Just nod your head if you understand."

She nodded.

"I met your ex-husband, Russell."

"Russ."

"Please, just listen."

She nodded.

"Russell told me what happened that evening with Lana. He kept you out of it. Completely out of it. Do you understand?"

She nodded.

"Tomorrow morning, he'll sign his statement. I'd like you to come in and give a statement, too. You can say whatever you want, or you can say nothing. But I'd like you to be there. Come early, seven o'clock would be good. The police station on Beretania Street. You know where that is?"

She nodded.

"Take a taxi."

She nodded again.

"And don't tell your husband."

She shook her head. "I would never tell him."

He turned to leave.

"I don't wanna go. It's too early."

"If he ever meant anything to you, if you loved him once, if for just a while a part of you felt happy and complete because he was in your life, then come tomorrow morning."

Sara looked up at him, her mouth half open, as if caught between thought and speaking.

All he could do was ask. He turned to go.

"How does he look?" She said softly.

Kai shrugged since he had nothing to compare him to. "He's healthy, but the years have been hard on him."

"Did he quit? Smoking, I mean?"

"No."

"He owes me a *papillon*." She smiled, closed her eyes, and nodded off to sleep.

Ka'ena followed him to the foyer. "Do you think she'll remember?"

"I don't know. She may or she may not or she could decide not to come."

He walked to his car and got in. She leaned in the open window. They were close enough he could have turned his head and kissed her. It was hard leaving her in this spider's nest.

"Think about my plan."

"You're fourteen."

"I won't be fourteen forever."

"You know, I'm the first person they'll come looking for you."

"I'll hide out for a while."

"It's not a good idea." He started the engine.

"Can I come tomorrow morning?"

"Not if it's gonna make you late for school."

"There's plenty of time. School doesn't start until eight-thirty."

'I doubt that,' he said with a look.

"Okay, eight. But the first thirty minutes is homeroom."

She stretched her fingers out, lightly brushing his shoulder, and stepped back from the car.

He drove out the gate.

Maybe it would be best for her to run away to the mainland. Living in that house—how had she survived? She'd said she had nightmares. She was sleeping perfectly fine next to him that morning. She seemed happy. He seemed happy.

But why had Sara married Osterlick? Did he have something on her that forced her to divorce Russell and marry him? The one piece of evidence that would tie her to the murder?

Kai headed for Mānoa. Grandma Osterlick had shown him the garage with a dozen or more boxes crammed around Osterlick's old 'Cuda. He wanted to look in those boxes. She'd let him, and she had the right to authorize his looking. And anything they found would still be admissible in court. But he couldn't do the search alone. Osterlick could find reason to have whatever he found ruled inadmissible and would distort and pervert his relationship with Ka'ena to do it. He needed someone to do the search, someone respected and unimpeachable.

He called the Crime Lab.

"Crime Scene Investigation. Sergeant Morris. How can I help you?"

"Detective Ahuna-Aki," Kai said and gave his badge number. "I've got a dozen banker boxes that need a going over. I'm looking for evidence in a murder investigation."

"What's the case number?"

Kai gave the old case number.

"Whoa. That number's fifteen years old."

"That's right."

"What are we looking for?"

"I'm not sure."

"What does it say on the warrant?"

Kai was silent.

"You've got a warrant, right?"

"I've got the property owner's permission."

"You run this by the PA on the case? Why am I even asking? You didn't, did you?"

"I spoke to Adler this morning. We talked about probable cause."

"Adler, huh? Usually I get the request for a search from your lieutenant. Have him give me a call."

"I was trying to wrap this up this weekend."

"This weekend? Nothing's happening this weekend. The soonest I could book you would be Tuesday or Wednesday, unless it's an emergency, and a fifteen year old case doesn't sound like an emergency. Call your lieutenant."

The line went dead.

Call your lieutenant. Coelho was the last person he'd call.

Why was Coelho the last person he'd call? He didn't know what they'd find. Coelho may be the only person who knew what to look for—if there's anything to find.

He scrolled through his contacts and tapped Coelho's cell number.

It rang four times before Coelho answered. "What?"

"I need your help to do a search."

"You've got to be kidding me. Who?"

"Osterlick's mother's garage. There's about a dozen boxes."

"You don't get it, do you? Shut this down. Now. You are seriously pissing me off. And you're pissing Osterlick off. And that should scare you."

It should, but he was so far out on the limb nothing seemed to matter. He had no ammunition to convince Coelho, no compelling argument. And it was Coelho who had sent those four thugs to work him over. Maybe calling him was a mistake.

"Where you at?" Coelho asked.

"In Mānoa. Osterlick's mother's house."

"Be there in an hour, in front of her house."

32

Kai had to decide. Was calling Coelho a mistake? Would Coelho call Osterlick? Or his goon squad? It occurred to him that Coelho hadn't asked for an address or directions—he'd been here before.

He parked half a block away but in a location from which he could watch Grandma Osterlick's house. He was waiting for Coelho but was looking out for off-duty cops. He didn't want to be ambushed the way he'd been the day before outside Pereira's house. It was a quiet street with little vehicular traffic and almost no pedestrians.

After an hour, Coelho's black Mustang pulled into the spot in front of the Osterlick house. Coelho got out, leaned on his car, and looked both ways up the block. Kai waited a few minutes to be certain more cars weren't following. He started his engine and drove over to the spot across the street from Coelho's.

He grabbed a small daypack with evidence collection materials and crossed the street to Coelho.

"Why are we here? I told you to shut this down."

"Osterlick has something on Sara Iwamoto. Where would he keep it? At his office? No. At his home in Kahala where Sara might run into it? Not likely."

"In his mother's garage?"

"It's worth a look."

"Why do we care?"

"Because it's evidence of a crime, and what we do is solve crimes—not cover them up."

Coelho spat on the ground. "Please, stop the noble speech before you make me puke. I've heard it before. Hell, I've probably told it. It's bullshit. And if you still believe it you're stupider than I thought."

Kai spat a few feet further but didn't respond. They walked side by side up the path to Grandma Osterlick's home. Kai rang the bell and somewhere inside the house the yappy dog answered. In a moment the old woman came to the door.

She looked Kai over and her face indicated this time she remembered him. "You came back." Then she turned to Coelho and scowled. "You?"

"Hello, Mrs. Osterlick," Coelho said. "We'd like to look in your garage, if you don't mind."

She pointed to the side of the house and closed the door. Kai and Coelho put on latex gloves as they walked to the side of the garage. After several moments the old woman and her yappy dog joined them from the house. She handed the key to Kai and he unlocked the side door of the garage. He felt next to the door for the light switch. A single bulb mounted to the center of the ceiling came on and cast a dim amber light.

Kai stepped in and squeezed his way to the front of the car where the boxes were stacked.

Behind him, Coelho let out a low whistle. "Look at that bad boy." His eyes were tracing the lines of the orange and black car. "Barracuda," he said, savoring the word. "I'd forgotten about his sweet ride."

Kai lifted down the top box. It was heavy and densely packed. He wanted to set it on the car hood, but with Mrs. Osterlick there and Coelho drooling over the car, he put the box on the floor. He pulled off the lid. Clothes—kid's clothes suitable for a young girl. He went through it, item by item, replaced everything, and closed up the box. He took down the next box and put it on top the first and repeated the process.

Coelho opened the door to the Barracuda and slipped behind the wheel. He ran his hands across the top of the steering wheel. He reached over to the glove compartment and looked through its contents. "Get me a bag. A big one."

Kai removed a large evidence bag from his kit and sidled to the open car window. Coelho held an evidence bag by one corner. He took Kai's bag and slipped his smaller bag inside. He closed the seal, signed his name, and filled in the location, date and time.

"I think this is what you want." Coelho held the bag so Kai could see the contents of the inner bag. A pair of scissors of a type a seamstress might use. "Let's get out of here."

Kai returned the boxes to the stack. Coelho was out of the car and exiting the garage. "Give the lady a receipt," he said over his shoulder as he walked to the front yard. Kai prepared a receipt for Mrs. Osterlick, and a form authorizing the search. He tried to hurry the process but the old lady asked him to explain what she was signing. As he was walking to the front he heard Coelho's Mustang start up with a roar. Coelho gave him a little smile and a wave and peeled away from the curb.

33

Kai watched Coelho drive away with the only piece of evidence they were likely to find. He'd just been played. Coelho could bury the scissors so deep they would never see the light of day.

He leaned against his car, suddenly out of energy. He was tired of playing catch-up, always being behind the curve. He drove home and parked nose-out, as always—ready to run away, as always. He climbed the steps to the second floor and unlocked his door.

The apartment was gloomy in the fading late afternoon light. He looked in the refrigerator. He'd drunk his last beer. He was out of coffee too. There was an open box of donuts. He put it on the table and sat in the lone chair. He looked at the sofa, his pillow at the far end. He'd slept there two nights ago. The dent in the pillow from his head was gone. Why would it be gone?

He looked around the apartment, starting with the table. The box of donuts. He opened it. Eight donuts remained from a box of twelve. He had one at Walt's, and Walt had taken one but didn't eat it. That one went in the trash. When he got home he opened the box to have a donut and coffee—but there was no coffee, so he didn't have a donut. Did the girl have a donut? He'd put his hands over his eyes. She could have taken one. He felt her behind him. She'd put her hands on his shoulders, massaged his neck. No, she didn't take one. There should be ten donuts, but there were eight. Someone had been in here. They'd tossed the room, did a good job but not real good. They'd put the pillow back dented side down and taken two donuts—had there been two of them? Coelho and another person?

Did they take anything else? What else had been on the table? The yearbook and the single photo of Lana—but he'd taken them with him when they went to the library and should still be in his car. He saw Ka'ena's skateboard standing on end by his surfboard. Had she brought anything else with her? He remembered Osterlick's words—given enough time he could find evidence putting the two of them in a compromising position.

The bikini bottom. He'd told her to take them with her. And she said to keep them, put them on his pillow. He checked the bedroom—nothing on or under the pillow. He picked up the pillow on the couch, moved the sheets. They weren't there. Had she taken them with her? Were they in her hand walking out the door? He didn't see them. She'd left them here, probably on his pillow just as she said. And now they were gone.

Was it Coelho who'd gone over the place? Was Coelho right here when he'd called him? Kai had been out of his apartment for more than a day—plenty of time for someone to give the place a thorough going over.

In his mind he saw the white triangle and loose strings of the bikini bottom. He'd felt the soft material, small enough to fit in his hand when balled up.

And now they had it—whoever they were. Coelho? Would he take them to Osterlick or run his own little game?

He felt like he was in an elevator that was dropping too fast.

34

Monday

Kai rose from the couch and crossed the apartment in the aqua half-light reflected from the pool onto the ceiling. He'd only slept sporadically through the night and decided to give up the effort. He showered, shaved, and dressed. He put on his best aloha shirt—this may be his last day on the job. He didn't expect a lei.

Going out the door he picked up Ka'ena's skateboard and carried it down to his car. Why hadn't Coelho taken it? Maybe he hadn't realized it was hers—not a girl's toy. He didn't know Ka'ena.

The parking lot of the Beretania Street station was mostly empty. The recruiters weren't yet at their post outside the authorized personnel entry. They'd show up just before change of shift, chat up the tired cops heading for their cars, take them out for breakfast, then return for the next change of shift. He avoided the lobby and the inevitable dirty looks he'd most likely get while waiting for the elevator.

He took the stairs to the second floor and entered the detective squad room. It was dark and empty. He turned on the florescent lights and found his way through the thirty L-shaped cubicles to his desk. An empty bankers box sat on the surface next to an application for the Baldwin Police Department.

He called the holding cell to have Russell Reynolds brought to the Detective Squad. He started his computer and opened an email with an attachment. Reynolds' statement had been transcribed and was ready to be signed. He sent it to the printer and crossed the empty squad room to retrieve the pages.

Back at his desk he went through the drawers checking for personal items to put in the bankers box, and found none. He pushed the box aside.

A uniform cop escorted Reynolds to Interview Room A and left him there before taking up a position outside the door. Kai gathered up the pages of the statement and entered the room. Reynolds was seated at a table, his back to the door, and facing the one-way observation glass. He wore a one-piece orange jumpsuit with OCCC stenciled on the back. The jumpsuit was crumpled from laying on his cot or the floor of his cell. Gray stubble was noticeable on his chin and dark half-circles drooped under his eyes.

Kai sat opposite him. He pushed the pages across the table. "Read this. If you're okay with it, sign and date at the bottom of each page."

Reynolds took the statement and went through it quickly. "Got a pen?"

35

Kai removed the cap from a blue Rollerball and put it on the table.

Reynolds looked up and their eyes met. His face mirrored the anger and disappointment Kai felt. The older man signed the pages and pushed them and the pen to the center of the table. Kai gathered them up and went to the door. "I spoke with Sara yesterday."

"She wasn't there."

"She says you owe her a *papillon*."

"She remembered," he breathed out in a sigh.

"*Papillon*. That's a butterfly, right?"

Reynolds turned to him. "It's a pastry—shaped like a butterfly, sort of. Right after giving birth to Lana, she was struggling to get the weight off. There were these little cake-like things that she'd fallen in love with when she was pregnant. At the same time I was trying to quit smoking. The deal was if I bought a pack of cigarettes I had to buy her a dozen of those *papillons*. I guess I owe her about a million of them."

He's still trying to keep promises he'd made to her fifteen years ago—fifteen long years without her. This guy really loves her. Kai left the room.

Kai went into the adjacent observation room and watched Reynolds. The papers Kai held in his hand would put Reynolds in prison for a long time. If they had gone straight to the cops fifteen years ago Sara would have been out by now and Reynolds would have been free to raise Ka'ena—that's if she'd been conceived. Instead they'd done something stupid. Hiding the body made it worse. A half decent attorney could have argued the affirmative defense of manslaughter, and claimed she was under extreme mental disturbance when she discovered her daughter was pregnant. They didn't know the law and tried to cover up what was done—and the cover-up is always worse than the crime.

Too bad they hadn't consulted a lawyer.

What if they had consulted a lawyer? And the only lawyer they knew was that nerdy guy from high school. They didn't know him well enough to have his home phone number, but they'd heard that Martin Osterlick was an attorney for the city. And they contacted him at work.

Kai returned to his cubicle, and dialed the number for PAPA.

"Prosecuting Attorney Paul Adler."

"I need a phone dump."

"You need a warrant, and you need probable cause to get it."

"Right, but that's for a private person. What about a city government line?"

He could hear Adler fidgeting on the other end. "I don't know. What number are you talking about?"

Kai recited back Adler's number.

"Is this a joke?"

"From fifteen years ago. The person who sat at your desk at that time."

"A prosecuting attorney?"

"A public worker."

"Pam Lo. You figured out who it is."

"That's right."

The fidgeting intensified. "I'm. Not. Sure." Tapping, rustling of papers. "I have to check with my boss when he gets in."

"Do you keep those records?"

"I'm sure somebody keeps them. I'll call you back."

He hung up the phone. The elevator pinged as the doors opened. Ka'ena took a step out and scanned the room. One hand blocked the door from closing as if she might need to get out in a hurry. Sara Iwamoto stepped from the shadow of the elevator and stood next to her daughter. The two women, side by side, were close in appearance despite the thirty-three year difference in age. Sara, in a long simple dress, was sophisticated and mature, but decidedly scared. Ka'ena, an inch or two shorter, with the same dark hair but with a wave, was dressed in her pleated navy skirt and white blouse school uniform. Ka'ena, innocent and confident, nodded her head towards Kai and took her mother's hand to guide her.

"Mrs. Iwamoto," Kai said as he rose from his desk. "Thank you for coming." He pointed to Interview Room B. "The shift is about to start. We'll have more privacy in there."

He had Sara sit in the chair facing the one-way glass. Ka'ena leaned against the wall behind her mother. He put Reynolds' statement in front of her. "You're husband signed this statement this morning."

"My husband? You mean my ex-husband." She lowered her eyes to the document. She read it, and read it through a second time. She raised her head. Her eyes were moist. "Russ is here?"

"Yes."

"Can I see him?"

"I can't let you talk to him, but—" he lowered his voice like he was about to break every rule in the book. "Come. I'll let you see him."

Kai led Sara and Ka'ena to the observation room between the two interview rooms. Sara looked at the man sitting at the table. He'd been there a while and was pushing particles of dust off the edge of the table—an activity of the bored.

"He looks older. Older than he should."

"He's had a few run-ins with the law—minor stuff. Jail, not prison."

"Can I talk to him?" Ka'ena asked.

He was ready to say 'no' but then thought it might get a reaction out of Mrs. Iwamoto. He opened the observation room door and let her out, nodding to the uniformed officer at the door of Interview Room A to let her in.

Kai and Sara watched Ka'ena enter the room. Reynolds looked over his shoulder to see who came through the door and quickly got to his feet. He opened his arms wide and she hugged him.

Sara put a hand to her mouth. "Lana. I've seen Lana hug him so many times. But Ka'ena, she's gone her entire life and never got a hug like that."

Kai watched as the girl buried her face in her father's shoulder. They stood that way for some time. No rubbing the other's back, no self-conscious actions. They just held each other.

After a while father and daughter let go. Ka'ena pulled a chair around so she could sit at a right angle to him. She put a hand on his, he put a hand on hers, she put a hand on top.

"Can we hear what they're saying?"

He could give her the earphones to listen in on the conversation in the next room but he didn't know what was being said. And her not knowing what they were saying might be a more powerful leverage than if she actually heard. "I can't do that." He escorted her back to her chair in Interview Room B.

Kai stood on the other side of the table. "I'd like you to tell me what happened that evening."

"You have my husband's—my ex-husband's statement."

"I'd like to hear it from you."

"I wasn't there."

"We are off the record. I haven't read you your rights. Haven't asked you to sign a waiver form." Kai was taking a chance. If a suspect talked without being Mirandized their statement could not be used in court. But if they confessed, they might truly feel remorse and be willing to repeat the confession after they'd been advised of their rights. It was a gamble.

"I was visiting one of my seamstresses."

"I know you were at home. We have the phone records. You called Martin Osterlick and asked for advice. He'd take a call from you. But from Russell? I don't think so." Kai was bluffing—he had no phone records. He didn't even know if he could get the records. It gets worse. If she didn't make a call then he just totally blew his credibility, and he'd get nothing more from her.

Her eyes were on his, no doubt trying to figure out what he really knew. The corners of her mouth turned down.

36

"He still loves you, ya know."

She looked down at the table. Kai thought she wouldn't answer. Several minutes passed before she spoke. "He said he'd *always* love me, back when we were in high school. I thought, how could he possibly know that?" She seemed lost in thought. "He said the same thing after the divorce."

"Tell me what happened," Kai said gently. It was not a question that could be dismissed with a 'no,' but a softly stated demand.

She didn't regard the request with any urgency as if she were telling him a dream she'd had the night before. "I was working on my spring collection—the most important one for the year because the summer collection would build off it. The previous year hadn't gone well and some stores weren't sure they wanted me back. Macy's, the big one for me, asked to see the whole line, not just sketches. They wanted something they knew would sell, but was different. I was working with a beautiful piece of material, but the layout was wrong. I'd already cut the material and it was ruined. I wouldn't get another chance. I thought by now I should be farther along in the collection—farther along in my career. I'd been doing this for fifteen years—ever since high school. I'd dropped out when I was in my seventh month with Chris, and I never finished.

"Lana was trying to talk to me, but I said 'could it wait?' It was such a beautiful piece of material, the texture, the pattern, the drape. But I'd cut it wrong and now there wasn't enough material. It was my fault, all my own fault. I should have paid better attention. Lana, my beautiful Lana, had to talk to me, but I didn't have the time.

"I was supposed to go to Parson's. It's a big design school in New York. I'd been accepted. I just needed to get my high school diploma. That was all I needed and I would be in the perfect place to start my career. But instead, I was trying to make something out of this beautiful cloth that I'd ruined. 'I'm pregnant,' Lana screamed, and then she laughed.

"I saw her hanging on to the edge of her dream for fifteen years, the way I was, but never living it. 'No, you can't be,' I said. She just laughed, this horrible, mocking laugh. 'So there, now I'm pregnant,' and she kept laughing hysterically. I told her to stop and I hit her. I pounded her in the chest. She stepped back and looked down at a spot just below her breast. I didn't realize the scissors were in my hand. She coughed, like she couldn't quite catch her breath.

"What had I done? It was no more than a scratch, but I'd never hit her before. I couldn't believe it. I don't think she believed it either. She went to her room. I tried the door but it was locked. She told me to go away. I should have opened the door right then, but I didn't. Not for another half-hour. And when I went in, the room was dark and she was so still. I said, 'we can figure it out together.' But she didn't move. There was no breath, no pulse. I took her hand. 'Come back,' I pleaded. 'We can still make something of this.' But I knew it was all over."

Kai put his hand on hers. She looked into his eyes, as if grateful for the understanding. He didn't really understand. He just wanted her to keep talking. "What happened next?"

"I called Martin. I knew him from high school and was certain he'd remember me—he kind of had a thing for me. I already had a boyfriend, Russ, but I knew how Martin'd felt about me. He was with the Prosecutor's office. He came over after work. He didn't even want to see Lana. He told me, hypothetically, if someone killed their daughter they might get fifteen years.

"Fifteen years. I'd already done fifteen years and I couldn't do it again. He said, just suppose a girl went missing, never to be seen again, the police would stay on it for one week, two at the most. The parents would grieve, yes they would grieve, but then they would move on and live their lives.

"I asked him how could he say this when he already knew. He said he could do this for me because he knew we shared a deep connection—or we could share one. I was sitting on the couch and he sat next to me and put his arm around my shoulder, pulling me into him as if to comfort me. And I let him.

"When Russ got home I told him what happened, but I didn't tell him Martin had been there. I said it was our only option. Otherwise I'd be gone for fifteen years. Russ loved me. He'd do anything for me."

"So you got him to bury Lana's body in the 'Ewa plain."

"It was his idea, but, yes, I got him to do it."

"And now he's going to take the full weight for you."

"Yes, I know."

"And Osterlick kept quiet."

"Yes. But it left me in his debt."

"So then you divorced Russell."

"Not at first. After all the media coverage died down, we tried to—I don't know—get back to normal. But it was harder on him. He felt it every time he came home, her empty place at the table, her favorite juice glass. And sometimes the way he looked at me, I didn't know if he hated me for what happened. He wanted to move away, go to California, start over. I couldn't stand the thought of starting over. For him it was different. He was a carpenter and could take his trade anywhere. I had to build a clientele. He went to look for work on the mainland. I didn't tell him I was pregnant. When he was gone six months, I moved out and filed for divorce."

"You went to Osterlick's mother's home in Mānoa."

"Yes, the little cottage, though his mother was never very nice to me."

"Osterlick paid the rent?"

"I had no money. I couldn't work. Ka'ena was difficult, even then. Martin worked it out with his mother. He would come by often—very often. I tried to keep it friendly but he was persistent. He wasn't Russ, and I may have said that to his face, and to a man, to say you are less of a man than someone else—he didn't take it well.

"He landed a job with Turner Carvalho and won a few big cases. He was the best in a courtroom. He did what he could to become Russ. He had his chin and jaw line improved, then hair plugs, and lipo. He worked out, ran a triathlon. But he could never, ever become Russ.

"So he offered me something Russ never could. Martin had the influence to help me get into boutiques. He could help my business if I—this is going to sound terrible." She turned her head away. "On condition I marry him."

"Did he help you?"

"He got me into boutiques, even another shot at Macy's. But after a couple of seasons it was obvious. Nobody wanted my collections because—" She took a deep breath and let it out. "My designs just weren't what people wanted. And so it became a hobby." She squeezed her eyes shut and shook her head—as if she'd known all along she'd never live her dream.

"Every day I wake up in prison. A gilded prison."

"You could divorce him."

She shook her head. "He would eviscerate me. Destroy me. Cripple me. Nobody, nobody betrays him and gets away with it. *Nobody*."

"Tell me—," He wanted to ask about the girl but wasn't sure how. "Tell me—."

"You want to know about Ka'ena. Martin never adopted her, never really acknowledged her. She's like Russ, in so many ways. Stubborn. Able to endure so much. And she feels things deeply." Sara looked across the table at him. "She doesn't make friends. She's only known you a few days, and she likes you. I'll use that word because she's fourteen and too young to know what love feels like. What I'm trying to say is, if you're going to let her down, do it soon, so she doesn't get too—I don't know the right way to put it. She's been let down too much already. I've let her down."

"When Martin went to work with Carvalho—you were okay with that?"

"I had no control over that. It was a good career move for him."

"But Carvalho. The son? His party? Your daughter?"

"Sure, Lana knew Richie from West Side Story. She went to a party at his house. So what? It's a small island."

Sara didn't know what happened at the party. She hadn't made the connection with the party and Lana getting pregnant. "She never told you about the party?"

"I'm sure she had a good time. She was so popular at school—right from the start."

"Something happened at the party."

"What do you mean?"

"A group of kids—boys, girls. They got her in a room."

"What?"

"Your daughter was raped, multiple times. That's how she got pregnant."

"No, that's not possible. Chris, her big brother was there. He'd watch out for her."

"He set it up."

She shook her head.

"During the investigation when Lana went missing, Osterlick found out about the party. He kept it quiet, and a year later he got a job at the father's law firm. Not just a job, a partnership."

"He said it was his experience."

"He knew what happened to your daughter and by whom, and he used keeping it quiet as a stepping stone."

"And the people responsible?"

"He let them get away with it."

"So he could make partner."

"That's the way it looks. You'll have to ask him."

"It sounds like Martin." She looked away from him, at the table, at the walls, anything but make eye contact. She seemed to be analyzing her options.

What does a mother feel when she finds out her daughter was raped and the boys responsible will never see justice? And the one who shielded them was her own husband, the man she slept with every night. And he did it for his own personal gain. Her gain too, since she lived off his wealth. Was this hatred for Martin or self-loathing for what she'd done? What does a mother do when she realizes she's been manipulated? The worst possible tragedy used by the man who'd sworn 'for better or for worse.' Revenge? What revenge would be great enough? Penance? How could one ever reach atonement for what she did to her daughter—her daughters?

"I want to make a statement."

Kai reached into a drawer on his side of the desk and retrieved a form and placed it in front of her. "You have the right to remain silent—"

37

"Do you understand your rights?" Kai asked.

"Yes," Sara Iwamoto said. "I'd like to write out my statement. Can you give me a pen and paper?"

He reached into the drawer and removed a pad of statement forms and a pen.

"And if you would give me a moment alone."

"Alright," he said as he stood. "I'll check back with you in fifteen minutes." He left the interview room and went directly to the adjacent observation room.

He opened the door and saw Ka'ena leaning on the sill of the one-way glass, headphones covering her ears.

"How much did you hear?"

"Most of it," Ka'ena said, pushing back the headphones.

He leaned on the sill next to her, shoulder to shoulder, peering out the glass in front of them, just like when they were in the car.

"Do you think she'll rat out dickhead? Say he advised her to hide my sister's body?"

"I don't know. If she wants revenge on Osterlick, but it's too late to affect tomorrow's election. The mail-in ballots have already been cast."

Ka'ena was quiet for a few minutes. "She might just follow my dad's story."

"She might."

They watched Sara Iwamoto write, scratch out, and write some more. She was on her third page, but large parts had been thoroughly blacked out. There was no telling what story she might tell, if it would help Russell Reynolds or let him take the full rap. She could implicate Osterlick in covering up the rape of Lana, but that would result in a he-said-she-said stalemate. The only innocent person in this whole mess was Ka'ena, and she was guaranteed to pay a price—no matter what the outcome.

"Tomorrow's the election," she said. "Are you going to vote?"

He hadn't planned on it—what was the point? "I hear he's already won from the mail-in ballots alone."

"I guess. But I'd vote against him if I could."

As tough as she was she was naïve enough to think voting gave her power. When would that change? How long will it take to beat that innocent notion out of her system? Will it be accomplished by the time she's old enough to vote? But then all her weapons were dramatic, shocking, and ultimately ineffective. Her sailor's mouth, her promise or threat of sex, her lies and deceptions—without these she had no weapons at all. But she had overcome four brutish, violent men beating the crap out of him simply by holding up her iPhone. They'd backed off, the way cowards do when they've been pointed out and exposed. Maybe that was her strength, her weapon—her demand for the truth, hot and searing, and she used it to cauterize the wounds of the past.

"Someone searched my apartment. I think it was Coelho."

His eyes were on hers in the reflection of the glass.

"Did you leave something—?"

"The bottom half of my bikini," she whispered.

"Where?"

"Under your pillow, in the living room."

"He took it."

"The perv." She was silent for a moment. "Shit. Will it get you in trouble?"

He couldn't answer.

"It will, won't it?"

She leaned a little to the left, he leaned a little to the right, until their shoulders were barely touching. The hair on his forearms stood on end in alert pattern. If he turned to her she'd turn to him and he'd have to address that she was fourteen and he was thirty. He'd have to think about letting her down easy, and he wasn't ready to do that. He wasn't ready for any of the possible outcomes. He just had to keep moving ahead.

"She's done."

Sara Iwamoto had stopped writing and was reading and rereading the pages she'd written. Kai pushed away from the window and left the observation room. He entered Interview Room B and sat across from Sara. She continued to hold the papers, reluctant to turn over three handwritten pages that would change the course of her life.

"I could use a drink," she said, and handed him the statement.

With many of the paragraphs crossed out there was just a little over a page of printed text. He read it through twice. "You left something out."

"It was the only way. I won't implicate Martin."

"Do you love him?"

She gave him a look that said, "Oh, please."

"Then why?"

"I couldn't say anything about Martin. He would come after me, after Russ, after Ka'ena. He'd especially come after you. This is the only way I can hurt him, by taking away something he really wants—me."

"You're willing to go to prison to do it?"

"I'm already in prison."

He understood. She was setting herself free of the fifteen year sentence—the guilt she'd carried around every day, every moment, and every time she tried to get close to a child that looked just like the one she'd killed. "I'll have this typed up and you can sign it. Then I'll arrest you. You'll be arraigned tomorrow, the same time as Reynolds. You should have an attorney. Do you know any—other than your husband?"

She shook her head.

"I'll bring Ka'ena in. She can sit with you for a while." Ka'ena was at the door by the time he reached it. She brushed past him and sat by her mother. Kai crossed the squad room to the civilian clerical staff's desk. He stapled the pages together and put a sticky on the top and wrote, "Type up ASAP. Mahalo. Kai."

Detectives were drifting into the squad room. It was nearly eight. Coelho wasn't in his office yet. Kai sat at his cubicle and assessed what he'd accomplished this weekend. He destroyed this girl's family, sending both natural parents to certain prison terms, probably until her early twenties, at a minimum. He'd torched his own career in the process.

Coelho entered the squad room and stopped at the door to his office when he saw the uniform officer outside Interview Room A. He went into the observation room just long enough to see who was in each interview room. He nodded to Kai to meet him in his office.

Kai followed Coelho into the small cluttered room. His lieutenant sat behind the desk and pointed at a chair for Kai.

"You were warned," Coelho said in a sing-song. "You were warned."

"Yes, sir."

"That's it? Don't you have anything to say for yourself?"

"If you want me out of here I'll get out. But I can't leave the way things are. The OIS Board signed off on the shooting, but you haven't released my service sidearm or my personal weapon back to me."

Coelho kept his eyes on Kai while he reached into his top desk drawer and removed a 9 mm Smith and Wesson and the small Taurus .380 TCP. Both guns were racked open and long, black zip ties were threaded through the barrels and the ejection ports, ensuring the weapons were clear.

Kai picked up the weapons. He checked the magazines—empty—and slipped them back into place. He withdrew a small folding knife from his pocket, cut and removed the zip ties, and released the slide locks. He stuffed the S & W into his waistband and the Taurus into his pocket. "I also need a favorable performance review."

"Why?"

"Without one I'll never get hired. I've been under your command for ten months. I just closed a fifteen-year-old open unsolved case."

Coelho nodded. "I'll keep that under consideration. The review will be on your desk by the end of day. You can agree or disagree with the points."

"What kind of a review might I expect?"

Coelho chuckled. "Why exemplary, of course."

This sounded too easy. Way too easy. Was Coelho planning something or had he passed the bikini bottom on to Osterlick? The two men stared at each other across the desk. "The scissors you found?"

Coelho reached into his briefcase and the evidence bag dropped onto the desktop with a *thunk*. "Yes, the scissors." He smiled. "You got confessions from both of them. We don't need the scissors to make a case against them."

Then who could he use the scissors against? The cover-up is always worse than the crime. "Osterlick."

"It gives me a little bit of leverage over him. Why had he held on to them? To put the squeeze on Sara. His keeping them proves he knew she'd killed her daughter—conspiracy to hide evidence of a felony. Even if it couldn't be proven in court it might be enough to have him disbarred. I don't know if there's a requirement that a prosecutor be bar certified. I think I'll hold on to this for a while."

"I believe you took something from my apartment."

"Me? You're mistaken. I've never been to your apartment."

"Yesterday afternoon. And you helped yourself to donuts while you were there."

Coelho reached into his briefcase again. He held an evidence bag by the corners, the white fabric plumping up the quart-size bag. "Trophy?" Coelho laughed and held it out to him.

Kai reached for the bag but Coelho pulled it back.

"I'll hold on to this too."

38

Kai picked up the typed statement from his desk and read it through. He carried it into Interview Room B and put it on the table in front of Sara Iwamoto. "Look this over. If it's okay, sign and date each page."

As Sara finished each page, Ka'ena took it from her and read it. "Mom, are you sure?"

"This is what you wanted. The truth."

"The whole truth," Ka'ena corrected.

"This is as close as I can get—for now. It's enough to get both of us out of that house." She turned to Kai. "You see, Martin never adopted Ka'ena. He is not her legal guardian and has no parental rights."

Kai realized Sara Iwamoto was looking out for Ka'ena too. Freedom came at a stiff price—prison for Sara and a group home for her daughter.

"I'll have to inform Child Welfare Services," Kai said. "She'll go into the system. First Kau Hale o Na Keiki for teens, then possibly foster parents."

"You have experience with this?"

Kai nodded. "I was in a group home when I was fifteen. I had a few cracks at foster families but they never worked out."

"I'll live with you," Ka'ena said to Kai.

"No," her mother said. "I don't want you ending up pregnant before you finish high school."

"I'm not stupid. I know how to not get pregnant."

"Break the curse the girls in our family seem to be under."

"I'm not like you and I'm sure not like Lana."

"I don't want you to throw your life away because you're hot for a boy. You can reach your dreams."

"I don't have dreams, remember? I have nightmares."

"I'm sure Detective Kai is a very nice person but he can't be your boyfriend. He's too old, for you I mean. And you're too young to have that kind of boyfriend. Besides, when Martin finds out what he's done Detective Kai had better be on a plane out of town. Ka'ena, you have to promise me, you'll let a good family foster you so you know what proper parenting is like, not what you've been getting. If you don't promise, I won't sign these papers and we'll both go home tonight."

Ka'ena crossed her arms and stared down her mother. "Fine."

"You promise?"

"Yes, I promise."

Sara took the papers and signed them.

Kai picked them up from the table. "I'll have a female police officer come in and pat you down and bag your personal possessions. Then I'll formally arrest you. They'll take you to a detention center in Kailua for today and bring you back to town for arraignment tomorrow. The prosecutor will ask for bail. If you can make bail, or if Osterlick puts it up for you, you can go home tomorrow. And so can Ka'ena."

"Once I'm out of his house, I'm never going back," Sara Iwamoto said.

"Me neither."

Kai left the room and called the duty sergeant to request a female officer to help him with the arrest procedure. A few minutes later a young female officer reported to him and together they went into Interview Room B. She performed the pat down just as the academy trained her to and escorted Sara to the elevators. Kai informed the uniform officer outside Interview Room A to take Reynolds back to holding.

Kai and Ka'ena watched as both parents, with their uniformed escorts, waited for an elevator to arrive. They stood face-to-face—their first encounter in fifteen years. They got into the elevator and were out of sight.

Ka'ena continued to stare at the closed elevator doors. She was now without parents. He couldn't guess what was going through her head based on his own life, she was a very different person. She glanced up at him and looked away.

"I'll call Child Welfare." He led her to his cubicle and she sat on the end of the desk. He pulled up the number and punched it in.

After several rings a voice came on the line. "Department of Human Services, Child Welfare Services. How may I help you?"

"Detective Ahuna-Aki, badge number 700914. I have a fourteen-year-old female child, both parents have been arrested—"

"Please hold." Hawaiian music came through the earpiece then abruptly stopped. He expected to hear another voice but the phone's LED screen showed the call had ended.

He redialed. The line was busy. He hung up.

"Do you have any relatives you're close to?"

She shrugged. "A grandma on the Big Island. But I never see her."

"Come on. I'll take you to school. We'll work out the Child Welfare part later."

They took the stairs down and went out the back entrance to the parking. They got into his car.

"My skateboard. You remembered."

He pulled onto Beretania Street and headed towards St. Teresa's.

"It's past eight. I'll be late."

"Maybe. Maybe not." He reached back and pulled the magnetic blue light to his lap. He rolled down his window and attached the light to the car's roof. He plugged its cord into the auxiliary power receptacle in the console and saw the reflection of the blue flashing lights in the rear window of the car ahead of him.

Cars opened up a space for them. They got on the freeway at Ward and Kai flicked on the siren. Code Three—lights and sirens. Cars ahead of them pulled to the right and they passed them quickly. They were doing eighty.

"This is so cool." She had a smile on her face.

He cherished that rare smile and wished the ride were longer. What was to stop them from continuing out to Makapu'u then circling the island Code Three?

They exited at Koko Head Drive and he flicked off the siren. He followed Wai'alae Avenue to St. Teresa's, pulled into the drive, and shut off the flashing blue lights. She strapped her skateboard to her book bag. They got out and walked side-by-side to the office.

Kai knocked on the Dean of Student's door. Dr. Jeffers looked up from her computer and waved them in.

"Good to see you again, Detective Kai," Dr. Jeffers said, her blue eyes glittering.

Ka'ena looked from Dr. Jeffers to Kai and back to Dr. Jeffers.

"Hello, Dr. Jeffers. Sometime today someone from Child Welfare will come to pick up Ka'ena. Both her parents have been placed under arrest."

"I don't understand."

"They're charged with the murder of her sister, Lana."

"Oh, I'm so sorry for you, Ka'ena. If there is anything we can do to help, please let us know."

"I want to keep coming here to school, but I don't know if my step-father will want to pay the bills."

"Don't worry about that. Tuition is paid in advance, so you're paid up for the rest of the school year. After that, we can look at scholarships."

"Thank you, Miss."

Dr. Jeffers wrote a note and handed it to Ka'ena. "Give this to your teacher to excuse your lateness."

"Thank you, Miss. Can Detective Kai walk with me to my classroom?"

Dr. Jeffers looked from Ka'ena to Kai and smiled. She nodded her consent.

Ka'ena pointed the way along the covered cloister. "The way she looks at you, I think she likes you."

"Don't nuns have to take a vow of abstinence?"

"I think I've just taken that kind of vow." She stopped walking and looked up into his eyes. "We could run away. You could kidnap me. We could live on Rabbit Island. They say there's a cave there—a lava tube where John Cummings hid guns to rescue the Queen."

"They'll hunt us down."

"Like Bonny and Clyde. We'll die in each other's arms."

"That's not how they died. Besides you're too young to die. You have so much more life to live. And I think you'll be good at it—you'll wring every juicy drop out of life."

"This sounds like you're saying goodbye."

"I guess I am."

"And we'll never ride around in your car again?"

He shook his head.

"So when they see me crying in the hallway they'll think it's about what's happened—when it's really about what didn't."

"That's what most regrets are—the things we didn't do but wish we had."

"You know that, but still you're going to go."

He had to go. If he stayed Coelho would have power over him, and Osterlick would destroy him in a public way so he'd never work again anywhere. At least now he had a shot at a small police force in Washington State. It was the safe thing to do. He had to take it.

"I wish we had kissed in the coffee shop," she said.

He couldn't explain to her why it would have been wrong because he couldn't explain it to himself. Some part of him had failed to grow past her age, either from fear or atrophy of those feelings. And some part of her had grown hard faster than her chronological years—under a source of unusual pressure. He knew it, most likely she felt it, but it could not be explained.

She dropped her eyes. "But I guess it's too late now."

"It's better this way."

She shook her head slowly. "No, it's not."

He took a step back.

She took a gulp of air.

He turned and walked to his car. He would never see this girl-woman again. In a way it was a relief. She was dangerous to be around. The feelings inside him were dangerous. The uncertainty of what she would do, and what he would do, were dangerous. He got back to his car and fumbled for the key. He got it into the slot and started the engine. He looked over to her seat—a small plastic red rose barrette.

39

Kai drove into the underground parking structure adjacent to the Police Department and found a space in the area designated for detectives. Looking between the parked cars he saw a young Asian woman in a beige polo shirt—the grad student working for Osterlick's campaign. He'd have to pass her to get to the lobby to take the stairs or the elevator.

 He slipped out of his SUV and closed the door quietly. He crouched-walked between the parked cars until a column was between him and the girl. Then he saw what he couldn't see before. Five rows of cars over stood two of the goons from his encounter on Saturday—the one with the baton and one of the younger off-duty uniforms. They were better concealed than Osterlick's campaign worker. So where were the other two? He'd have positioned them out of sight near the entry so they could spot their prey as he drove into the parking lot. If that were the case they'd be walking this way. He looked over his shoulder and saw the tops of the heads of two men several rows over walking with deliberation towards him. He crouched in front of a pickup truck.

The two men were weaving between the parked cars taking separate but parallel paths, getting closer. Kai stood directly in front of the trailing man, who stepped back and reached for his phone. Kai knocked it out of his hand. He reached for his side arm, a Smith and Wesson 5906. Kai knew this weapon well—it was identical to his own service weapon. As the man brought his right hand up with the pistol, Kai's left hand clasped the top of the gun pushing it safely to the side. His thumb depressed a button at the base of the trigger guard. The magazine dropped. Without a magazine the S & W could not be fired, even if there was a round in the chamber. The man grasped Kai's left hand. Kai's right hand seized his thumb and wrenched it sideways until it snapped. He pushed back on the gun's slide and depressed the detent pin, an action he took every day when he field-stripped his own weapon. The slide jumped forward a half-inch and Kai pulled it off the frame leaving his opponent holding a partially disassembled pistol.

Kai heard the older cop running towards him. He swung around and hit him in the face with the slide assembly. He was a big guy but was momentarily dazed by the blow. He grabbed Kai's shoulder. The man had a ballistic vest under his aloha shirt—no sense punching him in the torso. Kai brought his knee up sharply into the man's groin, then a second time and a third. The man bent at the waist and Kai slammed his head into the hood of the pickup truck. The car alarm went off.

The first man grabbed Kai from behind but Kai pulled one hand loose and twisted his arm till the man fell to his knees. Kai stepped over the arm and continued the twist until the man screamed and he was certain he'd dislocated the shoulder.

Kai pulled the S & W out from under the second man's shirt and removed the slide, dropping the frame to the ground. He put the two slides into the back pocket of his jeans. With the car alarm blaring the other two goons would know something was up and where. How they would react was the unknown. Kai crouched and ran between the cars towards the door to the elevator lobby.

The second off-duty patrolman stepped in front of him. His hand rested on the grip of his weapon still in its holster. Kai tackled him. The man struggled to free his weapon but Kai held his arm to his side and punched at his face with his right. He got in three good shots to his eye before the baton slammed across his back.

Baton Man jabbed the nightstick at Kai and pulled the trigger. Kai convulsed, and the sudden movement was enough to break the connection. Kai rolled to his feet on the other side of the downed officer. Baton Man swung the nightstick but Kai was backing away. They were in the last row of cars parked tail-in to the wall of the structure. Kai had no place to go.

Baton Man smiled. "Can't run now."

The business end of the baton came at him. When Baton Man hit the trigger a blue-white arc leapt across the inch and a half gap between the two electrodes. Baton Man stepped over his fellow goon. Kai picked that moment when he was just a little off balance. He deflected the baton and threw a punch at the big man's face. It was a glancing blow and the man swung the baton, but they were too close for Baton Man to use the effect of leverage. They were both stepping on or over the unconscious man and neither had good footing.

They were momentarily separated. Baton Man jabbed at Kai, who twisted and grabbed the man's right wrist. Kai pulled a nylon tether separating it from the baton—a disabling switch in the event the baton was taken away. The man poked the baton at Kai but it didn't discharge. He swung the baton but Kai dodged the blows. Baton Man took another desperate swing then reconnected the tether.

Kai jumped at him and grabbed hold of the baton with both hands, one hand clamped over Baton Man's trigger finger—the batteries couldn't last for long if continuously discharged. The electrodes spit out a hot blue-white arc but the baton was horizontal between them. They both had two hands on it. Kai pushed the stick towards him but Baton Man wore a ballistic vest that would insulate him from getting zapped.

Kai couldn't hold back Baton Man's extra weight and the bigger man pushed him down. Kai was slowly getting bent backwards over the hood of a car. It was as if he were bench-pressing three hundred pounds. "I'm gonna take this bat and shove it up your skinny ass." As the baton got closer to his face the crackle grew louder, the smell of ozone increased from the discharge.

Kai slammed his forehead into Baton Man's nose. Blood flowed from the big man's nostrils. Baton Man staggered a little but still held on tight to the baton. But Kai had won back a little space. He head butted him a second time and Baton Man cried out. Kai pushed the baton lower. He head butted him again and the baton went just below the waist. Kai pulled on the trigger end angling the baton at the man's crotch. The man jerked spasmodically. Kai's hand clamped over his trigger finger. The man dropped to the floor but Kai kept the pressure on his hand and the baton. Smoke rose from the man's lap where the electrodes singed the material.

He pulled the baton away. Baton Man stopped convulsing, his face frozen in a grimace. Blood bubbles blew and exploded from his nose onto his shirt, his eyes fixed on Kai.

He pulled the nightstick from Baton Man's hand and took the S & W from the hip holster. He removed the slide assembly and tossed the frame under a car. He got the pistol from the man he was standing on and disassembled it, keeping the slide assembly.

Baton Man tried to get up. Kai pushed the baton towards his face. The man recoiled in terror. A dark wet stain appeared on the lap of Baton Man's trousers and a small puddle spread out on the concrete floor under him. The air reeked of feces.

Kai staggered towards the lobby door, supporting himself on the parked vehicles. The car alarm still blared, alternating between honks and sirens.

He wiped his forehead — smeared blood on the back of his hand. His left sleeve was half torn off and the side of his shirt singed from the baton. His knuckles were raw. He couldn't stand in the elevator lobby looking like this.

He stood up straight and walked to the lobby door. The grad student's eyes went wide then looked down at the phone in her hand.

His hand went over hers. "You don't need to call him."

She looked up at him and swallowed. "Too late," she said in her high, soft voice.

He let go of her hand and she put the phone to her ear. "Yes, sir. It's Omi, sir. I'm sorry. I accidentally hit speed dial ... Yes, sir ... I will, sir."

Kai nodded his thanks and went to the stairs. His knees were wobbly and he pulled himself up by the handrail. He paused at the top landing to catch his breath. His heart was still beating too fast. He knew Osterlick would be in the room with Coelho. He didn't have a plan. He liked having a plan but he couldn't think. Shit, he could barely stand. He was going in. Why not? He'd burned all his other bridges.

He pulled open the door and crossed the lobby to the detective squad room. The civilian admin assistant looked up from her computer screen—her mouth dropped open. Detectives at their cubicles followed him with their eyes. The room went still except the soft squeak of his Asics on the floor. The window blinds of Coelho's office were pulled down and closed, but he could hear talking through the glass wall.

Kai put his hand on the knob and pushed the door open.

40

Kai stepped into the room.

Osterlick and Coelho fell silent and turned to him. Osterlick was standing. Coelho was seated behind his desk, his chair pushed back against the wall as if he were trying to get as far away from Osterlick as possible.

Kai dropped the stun baton and the four slide assemblies on the desk.

"What's this?" Coelho asked.

Kai said nothing.

Coelho looked him over. "What the hell happened to you?"

"Your goons."

"What are you talking about?"

"The four bulldogs you sicked on me Saturday and just now down in parking."

"I didn't send anybody after you, now or Saturday."

Coelho's surprise looked genuine. Could he have put this together wrong?

Coelho squinted at Osterlick. "What did you do?"

"I'm not afraid to take the necessary steps—"

"You had a police officer assaulted? One of my men?"

"He stuck his nose—"

"This thing's rated at five million volts," Coelho pointed at the stun baton. "It's illegal in this state, even for law enforcement. That's a felony. Get out of my office."

"You don't dismiss me."

"Get the fuck out."

"You should be careful," Osterlick said to Coelho with a little grin. "Things could come out. Certain things."

Coelho reached into his drawer and pulled out the evidence bag containing the scissors. "You're right. Certain things *could* come out. Remember these?"

Osterlick stared at the bag until he recognized the contents. "How did you get that?"

"The best possible way, with a consent to search the premises, signed by the property owner. Now whose fingerprints are we going to find on the original e-bag? Yours? That's what I'm guessing. I wonder what a little thing like that will get you? Lose your license to practice? Indictment for conspiracy?"

"Don't you fuck with me, Coelho."

The lieutenant jumped to his feet. "You don't fuck with me, or any of my men. Including Kai. Get out of my office you little shit."

Osterlick moved to the door but stopped in front of Kai. "I will settle with you."

Kai looked down on the little man and spit.

Osterlick wiped the bloody spittle off his face and marched out the door.

Seconds ticked off in silence as both men, Kai and Coelho, faced off. Kai wasn't sure where Coelho stood—if he could be trusted or not.

"You've made a powerful enemy," Coelho said softly. "He's gonna win the election tomorrow, it's a certainty."

"Looks like you're on his shit list too."

Coelho shrugged. "Politics. It comes with the territory. He just takes it to a new level where it could get deadly."

Kai was still shaky and he braced himself against the desk.

"Why don't you sit down?"

Kai sat in the chair across from Coelho.

"Tell me about these four guys."

Kai pulled out his phone and played the video Ka'ena had shot. "The two older ones—might be plain clothes. The other two, about my age, lots of gym time, looked like off-duty uniforms. They all had standard issue Smiths, and two of them wore vests. We'll know when they show up for roll call and don't have their service pieces. One may have a dislocated right shoulder and another a black eye. Oh yeah, one big guy's got a broken nose." He chose not to mention the electrical burn in the groin area.

"They may not be HPD. Could be Sheriffs, or work directly for the Prosecutor's office, or could be RIFed from HPD and making ends meet as investigators for Osterlick's law firm. I'll find out who they are. Send this to my number." Coelho picked up the phone. "Get a tech up here to collect four Smith and Wesson slides and a stun baton. I want to know who they belong to. Check fingerprints, serial numbers, whatever. Make this a priority. Start with law enforcement." He hung up the phone.

Something was nagging at Kai. "These four guys— Saturday they caught up with me at Chip Pereira's house. His widow made a call. I thought it was to you, but if you didn't send them she must have called Osterlick. So if she knew to call Osterlick, maybe Chip Pereira had a relationship with him—going back to when Lana went missing."

"I didn't know about it."

"I thought you'd scuttled the investigation."

"That investigation didn't need scuttling. There was nothing to go on. We looked, but nothing came up."

"Nothing? Plenty of stuff came up—like the fuck party where Lana was raped."

"She was raped?" Coelho shook his head. "I didn't know, I swear."

"Chip must have come across it and passed it on to Osterlick."

"I was going through a lot back then, a nasty divorce and custody thing. I thought I was handling it. Some days Chip covered for me, but I guess he was working for Osterlick."

"Or Osterlick had something on him."

"He digs up dirt, or manufactures it. Now he's got foot soldiers to do it for him. He casts his lines wide and deep. If there's something out there, some vulnerability, some past indiscretion, even the hint of a suspicion, he'll find it and use it."

"He's got something on you."

Coelho laughed. "You don't know what you're talking about."

"It must be something big. He's got his hooks in deep."

"You're blowing smoke."

"He just said, 'Things could come out.' What's he got?"

"Why should I tell you anything? What does it get me?"

"Maybe there's something I can do."

Coelho laughed. "You better save yourself first. But I appreciate the gesture. I really do." He reached into his desk drawer and put a file folder on the surface by his left hand and the e-bag with the bikini bottom by his right. "I'll give you a choice. Here's your evaluation—it's an excellent review. It couldn't be better if you'd written it yourself." He slid the folder into a Manila envelope and put it by his left hand. Then he indicated the clear zip-lock bag. "And here we have evidence a precocious fourteen-year-old girl was in your apartment. If we run this what will we find? A drop of semen? A little saliva?" He slipped the zip lock bag into a second Manila envelope and put it by his right hand. "You have a choice. Take one and the other stays with me. Without a good review no one will hire you. You couldn't get a job walking security at a mall. In HPD you'd get kicked down to patrol." He indicated the envelope under his right hand. "Or envelope number two. If this fell in the wrong hands you could be labeled a sex offender—sixteen is the age of consent in this state. Anything younger is a felony. But then that's only important if you're in the state."

Kai stood and looked at the two envelopes.

"Why don't you take a little time to think about it? Clean yourself up. Go home and get a new shirt. Come back after lunch and let me know."

Kai nodded. He opened the door but stepped back to the desk. "I've made my choice." He lifted one envelope off the desk.

"Are you sure?"

41

Kai went to his cubicle and made a call. A woman picked up. "Department of Human Services, Child Welfare."

"Detective Ahuna-Aki, HPD badge number 700914." He described the circumstances. A fourteen-year-old girl would need to enter the system, starting tonight.

"We're kind of busy over here," she said in a tired voice. He heard the clicking of a keyboard and the rustling of paper. "Mondays are always crazy," the voice said almost absent-mindedly. "People behaving badly—the parents I mean. And it always lands on the kids. Always the kids." More paper shuffling. "I've got a case worker who can do a field pick-up at six."

"Not till this evening?"

"That's the best I can do."

He agreed to meet the caseworker at Mānoa District Park, and gave his cell number just in case. He'd picked that park because it was across the street from Kau Hale o Na Keiki group home for girls. The location was kept secret, even from the police—some of the children had been taken from abusive family relationships, and some of those families, or extended families, included members of law enforcement. He knew the location because his sister had spent three years at the house.

Kai was still getting stares. He put the Manila envelope under his arm and walked to the Men's Room to wash his face and hands. There was a lot of blood on his face but very little of it was his. In the middle of his forehead was a strawberry colored lump. The front of his shirt was dark with blood and the sleeve was torn. His muscles were exhausted like he'd worked out his full body too intensely. He took the elevator down one floor to parking. The car alarm had been silenced. The grad student and the thugs were gone. He found his car. It was sitting low. All four tires had been slashed.

He called a tow company that did a lot of HPD business. They'd send a tow truck over in half an hour, the dispatcher said, bring it back to their shop on Queen Street and get new tires onto his rims. He sat in the car with the windows rolled half down and closed his eyes.

A few seconds later, there was a tapping on the window. The tow truck driver apologized for taking so long. He checked his phone—it had been an hour since he'd called. He slowly drove the car out of the parking structure so the driver could pull it onto the flatbed, and rode in the cab with him the few blocks to the shop. He fell asleep again in the waiting room, despite the noise of pneumatic impact wrenches, the blare of a wall mounted TV tuned to conservative yell shows, and the hard plastic chair. He paid with a credit card and drove home.

He took a shower and changed his clothes. He felt a lot better, and despite a cut lip and bruised cheek, and the bruise on his forehead, looked better. He checked the time—school would be letting out soon. He took the Manila envelope to the car and drove to St. Teresa's.

He waited at Dr. Jeffer's office. Her eyes skipped around the damage to his face and settled on his eyes. "Have you been fighting?"

He shrugged like a kid who'd been caught.

She shook her head then smiled.

"Child Welfare can't pick her up until six, so I'll take care of her till then."

"Yes, you should take care," Dr. Jeffers said in a way that suggested some special insight to the cosmic joke, that he should be careful taking care.

The final bell rang and the halls were suddenly full of girls moving quickly and excitedly to the exits. Ka'ena appeared in the doorway and leaned against the frame. "Will you be taking me to Child Welfare?" She was the girl again, the soft-voiced fourteen-year-old, with the thumb of one hand hooked in the shoulder strap of her book bag, and the other hand holding the tip of her skateboard.

"Thank you, Dr. Jeffers," Kai said.

"Take care, both of you."

They made their way through the crowd of girls to his car.

"You got in another fight," she said.

"Yeah. Same guys, different outcome."

"The guy with the stun gun?"

"I used it on him—fried his sausage and eggs."

"Good."

"And your day?"

"One of the nuns asked me about my weekend. I said, 'I met this cute boy. He took me to a bar where there was this huge fight—over me. Then I got naked and offered him my virginity. The next day a bunch of cops worked him over. I got to drive his car. We went to church on Sunday. I took him to meet my parents and he arrested them for murder. A fun weekend.' The poor lady was crossing herself and saying Hail Marys. I think she fears for my soul."

They got into his car and she saw the Manila envelope on her seat. She looked inside. "Thanks," she said, and stuffed the envelope into her book bag.

"They're coming for you at six at Mānoa Park. We've got some time. What do you want to do?"

"We could go to the beach. I've got half a bikini."

He didn't respond.

"Or we could go to church."

"You're a person of extremes."

"Is that good or bad?"

"It's different. Very different."

"Why don't we get something to eat and have a picnic in the park."

They drove to Starbucks and got a couple of sandwiches, and a coffee for him and a fizzio for her. At the park he led her to a large tree. They sat on the grass and ate.

"Which house is it?"

"Up a block. The white one with the chimney."

"It's big."

"Six bedrooms. Five girls and one for the overnight staff."

"What's it going to be like?"

"It's an emergency shelter—all the girls will be different. Could be runaways, abuse victims, homeless. They'll settle you in, help you get personal items from your old house—clothes, books, stuff like that. Long term they'll try to find you a permanent foster home."

"Did you like it?"

"The place I was at was different. I got into a lot of fights."

"You? Fights?"

"I was kind of a hardhead. If you go with it you can end up having a normal life."

"Normal? I don't want *normal*. That's the last thing I want."

"My sister was over there for three years. Now she's at Women's Community Correctional."

"Will you come and visit me?"

"I dunno. I'm not supposed to know where it's at."

"Say yes, even if you know you'll never come."

"We could meet under this tree. My sister and I used to meet here. We'd lay on our backs and imagine we could see the future"

"Could you see the future?"

"Not very well. We never saw the same things. I guess that part turned out to be true."

"You want to try it?"

He shrugged and laid back in the grass.

She laid back too. "Now what do we do?"

"Just stare up at the sky for a while, until your eyes go watery, then close your eyes, and see if anything comes to you. And no talking."

"Okay."

He stared up at the immense blue sky through the silhouetted leaves and branches of the Monkey Pod tree. A gentle breeze caused the light to flicker. The sky became a paler blue. His eyes watered and he closed them.

The darkness was a relief. It seemed to intensify as if he were in shadow. He felt a slight pressure on his lips lingering for several moments. He was certain it had been there only when it was gone. He dared not open his eyes not wanting to find out it wasn't true.

After a while he opened his eyes and turned to the right. Her empty Starbucks cup was lying on its side in the grass. She wasn't there. He sat up. Down the hill she was talking to a woman standing by a state motor pool car. He wiped the tears from his eyes.

The End

Acknowledgements

This book would not have been possible without the wonderful tutelage and friendship of Bill Bernhardt. Special thanks to Laurie Hanan who provided comments and encouragement from beginning to end. I would also like to thank those who read parts of the manuscript in progress and made valuable comments, including Kenneth Andrus, Gail Baugniet, Dani Brown, Dawn Casey, Daisey Chun, Bill Fernandez, Burke Holbrook, Nancy Holbrook, Dennis Lohr, Brian Malanaphy, Kent Reinker, Janet Rendall, Andy Scontras, and Lisa Scontras,

I would especially like to thank my wife Doris Christensen for her patience and understanding for putting up with me while these characters inhabited my head.

www.ingramcontent.com/pod-product-compliance
Lightning Source LLC
LaVergne TN
LVHW051358080426
835508LV00022B/2885